The Berkeley Guide to Employment
for New College Graduates

The Berkeley Guide to

Employment for New College Graduates

by James I. Briggs

in association with the staff of the
Career Planning and Placement Center
University of California—Berkeley

compiled and edited by
Robert B. Nelson

 Ten Speed Press

650.14
B85b

1

TEN SPEED PRESS
P.O. Box 7123
Berkeley, California 94707

Library of Congress Catalog Number: 84-51136
ISBN: 0-89815-136-8

Book Design by Hal Hershey
Cover Design by Brenton Beck

Printed in the United States of America

10 9 8 7 6 5 4 3 2 1

Library of Congress Cataloging in Publication Data

Briggs, James I., 1941–
    The Berkeley guide to employment for new college graduates.

    Bibliography: p.
    1. Job hunting—United States. 2. College graduates
—Employment—United States. I. Nelson, Robert B.
II. University of California, Berkeley. Career Planning
and Placement Center. III. Title.
HF5382.75.U6B74 1984   650.1'4   84-51136
ISBN 0-89815-136-8

Preface

This book is written to help you as a college student or recent college graduate in your search for work which is satisfying, meaningful, and consistent with your interests and educational background.

Its basic assumption is that the most important factors in the career planning and job hunting process are you and the personal effort you dedicate to this process.

To be successful in today's job market you will need to:

1. Define your career objectives as clearly as possible based on:
   a) an understanding of what it is you do well and enjoy doing given your education and life experience, and
   b) factual information about the world of work.

2. Plan and implement a well-focussed job search campaign that will lead to the realization of your career objectives.

Based on the accumulated experience and written materials of the Career Planning and Placement staff at the University of California, Berkeley, this book provides step by step advice on how to decide your own career directions and pursue and attain those career objectives that are most important to you.

We wish you every success in your quest.

Acknowledgements

This book is the result of the contributions of many. Thanks and credit are due them all.

First, to the members of the University of California, Berkeley, Career Planning and Placement Center career advising staff, present and past, whose ideas and materials formed much of the foundation for the original manuscript and whose individual contributions are much in evidence: Jane Adams, Rocky Boschert, Jackie Chapa, Mary Comendant, Peggy Dempsey, Liz Gish, Sandra Hagevik, Barbara Holloway, Suzanne Koehn, Jim Leinen, Linda Lewis, Leanna Luckey, Kathryn MacClelland, Jean Moe, Carey Olson, Barbara Rice, Michael Robinson, Priscilla Scotlan, Gail Sheridan, Marve Slavid, Kathleen Stanton, Jennifer Sugiyama, Jim Sullivan, and Robert Taylor.

Special thanks to Liz Gish, Leanna Luckey, Kathy MacClelland, Jean Moe, Marve Slavid and Kathleen Stanton, who reviewed the first several drafts and provided the support and encouragement to continue; to Barbara Rice, who prepared the excellent bibliography; and to Vera Ferris, my secretary.

Next, to Howard Figler, University of Texas, Austin, and Christopher Shinkman, Stanford University, admired colleagues and friends, who reviewed the manuscript as it neared its final revision and offered many helpful suggestions.

To Bob Nelson, author, humorist, and graduate student extraordinaire, who compiled the original manuscript and graciously helped revise, edit, and improve subsequent drafts; and to Alasdair Bowie for entering the final revisions to the manuscript.

To my wife, Kathy Gannon-Briggs, and our four children, Elizabeth, Eileen, Jennifer, and Julie, whose love, patience, and encouragement were essential to the completion of this project.

And finally to John Crystal, my early mentor in the field of career development, to Richard Bolles, and to all those who over the years have contributed directly or indirectly to the knowledge and skill my staff and I have developed in our strivings to assist university students in their quest for work that is meaningful, satisfying, and full of the rewards they seek.

James I. Briggs

Contents

CHAPTER *1*:

Finding Employment
in Good and Bad Times

Blue and Gold, 1891

You will be graduating soon, or maybe you have already graduated, and you are looking for a job. The pressure is on from many fronts—maybe from family, maybe from peers who have already been successful in finding work, maybe from yourself to show that you are worth something to somebody. Picking up this book is a great start since you are undoubtedly motivated enough to learn what you can do to increase your chances of success in finding work you want. Properly motivated, you have more control over your future job prospects than you may think you have. To begin with, you need to discard any myths you may hold about employment.

MYTHS ABOUT EMPLOYMENT

Sometimes people believe too much of what they hear about careers, employment, and job-hunting and, unfortunately, act accordingly. If they do venture to test these beliefs, it is often with half-hearted attempts that confirm their original beliefs and thus become self-fulfilling prophecies. Believing myths about career planning and job hunting is easy—especially when doing so leads you to the conclusion that things are out of your control. Consequently you can come to believe that no action on your part would seem to be able to change things.

Examine the following myths to see if there are some that you have come to believe and that may be having a negative influence on your thinking about career planning and job hunting.

Myth: Job market demand should be the primary determinant of academic and career choices. Selecting a major or pursuing a career just because it's "hot" in the job market can be dangerous. You may enjoy neither the coursework nor the job you get later. The careers in demand when you are a freshman or sophomore may not be in demand by the time you graduate. You are on much firmer ground when you select a major or choose a career goal that genuinely interests you. The job market demand tends to move in cycles. What is "hot" soon becomes "cold" as supply rushes to meet demand and vice versa. New career fields and jobs emerge every year as a result of changes in technology, public policy and economic trends. Factors that influence job market demand are frequently unpredictable.

This is a myth that many parents may also believe in. Anxious about your future and concerned about the financial "investment" they may be making in your education, they may put undue pressure on you to major in an area where a job after graduation appears to be a sure bet. This can lead to difficult conflicts if you feel inclined to pursue a career goal that your parents do not see as holding much future promise.

Myth: When you select a college major you choose a career. While it is true that certain majors such as engineering, computer science, and accounting prepare students for fairly specific career fields, a far greater number of majors do not have a direct correlation with given career areas. Liberal arts majors often find that they have a very wide variety of career options, including some in technical fields, because their backgrounds are so broad. Even within the technical or professional majors, where specific job skills are taught, there are many different kinds of jobs from which to choose. And remember your college education is much more than mere training for an entry-level job after you graduate.

Myth: Liberal arts majors are unemployable. Liberal arts graduates develop skills that are highly valued by employers and that are applicable to a wide variety of professional jobs. While these graduates sometimes take a bit longer to find the right opportunity, their potential for advancement beyond the entry level is usually very strong. In a longitudinal study of AT&T employees[*], humanities and social science majors were found to be stronger than engineering majors and similar to business majors in administrative skills and motivation for advancement. In the area of interpersonal skills, liberal arts majors were strongest of all groups. If these graduates sometimes take more time finding a "niche" in the working world, it's usually because they do not know what they can or want to do or they are not aware of the options available to them. (For more information on career options for liberal arts graduates, see Chapter Eight.)

Myth: There is little that counts beyond academic coursework when it comes to getting hired. Supplementary courses and independent study projects can be helpful as well. And often experience gained and skills developed through extracurricular activities such as student organizations, athletic teams, social groups, and student government count heavily in hiring decisions. Internships, summer and part-time jobs and volunteer activities play an important part in developing a greater understanding of yourself and the world of work. Such experiences are important in establishing professional contacts which are crucial to successful

[*]*Career Patterns: The Liberal Arts Major in Bell System Management*, by Robert E. Beck, published by the Association of American Colleges, 1981.

career growth. Employers consistently place a high value on these extra-curricular activities, internships, part-time and summer work experiences.

Myth: You cannot find a job when there is high unemployment. A logical belief to hold, right? If people are losing jobs, how can there be jobs to spare? There are always jobs available despite the state of the economy. Workers might get displaced and certain industries may be severely depressed, but there are almost always other opportunities. Even if the economy is not expanding, normal turnover and the need to replace people in existing positions create thousands of new opportunities each week. As a result people with skills and motivation are always in demand.

Myth: It's whom you know, not what you know. Personal contacts can and do play a part in any career. The myth comes in the belief that you don't know anybody. Or that those people you do know could not possibly be helpful to you. But whom you know is, to some extent, directly under your control. You can increase the number of people in your field that you know, and perhaps by doing so get to know one of the "right" people for you. You will also be surprised how many connections you can make through the people you already know.

Myth: If you are qualified, employers will seek you out. Even a good idea or a great product has to be sold. You have to get the word out that you are available and have something to offer that is of value and perhaps unique. Employers beat a path to few doors. Good job hunters seek out their preferred employer; they don't wait for employers to come to them.

Myth: Your first job will determine your career. In any decision involving competing choices where each possibility has its own advantages and disadvantages there is rarely one hundred percent certainty. Any choice involves some risk. Do not think that you cannot change your mind. Especially in the area of career choice, you are almost always free to explore new directions and make new choices as you learn more about yourself and various careers, through your experience. Young people in their twenties change jobs frequently and often change their career direction.

Myth: If you get more education, you will be more valuable. It is easy to avoid looking for work by simply going back to school, but you may face the same problems when you get another degree. The importance of more education varies from field to field. In some cases it can quickly lead some employers to think you are overqualified for your desired position. It is not uncommon for a job hunter with an advanced degree to take a position that the individual could have easily held with less education. Don't use education simply as a means of postponing the inevitable need to decide on a career direction and hunt for a job. Degrees cannot always be equated to jobs. However, if more education is required for you to pursue your chosen career, research and choose your academic program carefully to insure that what you will be learning will in fact help you to reach your specific goals.

Myth: If you do not have experience in the field, you are not qualified. Many students become frustrated by what seems to be an impossible maxim to break—namely, "You need experience to get a job and a job to get experience." It may not always be easy for those who are graduating from school or changing careers to persuade an employer to hire them without relevant experience, but it frequently happens. Those who are effective can parlay the variety of experiences they have had in their lives so far into marketable skills. They also sell themselves on the basis of personality traits such as initiative, honesty, creativity, and the willingness to work hard.

OVERCOMING THE DIFFICULTY OF FINDING A JOB

From these myths it is easy to see how people can come to believe that all the cards are stacked against them. There are, however, some factors that will give you the advantage you need. Here are four factors under your control which are imperative to any successful job search.

Imperative #1:

Focus. You must define for yourself a job objective which enables you to focus your job search. Too many job hunters go looking for "a job" without paying careful attention to defining what they are looking for. As a result, they tend only to scratch the surface of opportunities available and, because of their lack of focus, waste considerable time and effort chasing after openings more because the jobs are available than because of any personal commitment to the work or the organization. In short, your success in finding what you are looking for is directly related to your ability to define it clearly, based on what you know about yourself and the world of work. It should be your definition of what you, not someone else, believes is best for you.

Imperative #2:

Information. Information is power for the job hunter. Specific information about current openings is, of course, important. More general information about the career field, the organization, the work group, and specific individuals is essential to your career planning and job hunt. Resources are available from which you can obtain invaluable information which will sharpen your career focus, enable you to conduct an informed, professional job-seeking campaign, and allow you to make more informed selection decisions about employers with whom you might like to work.

Imperative #3:

Job-Hunting Skills. Knowing job-hunting skills is fundamental to any job search regardless of profession, level or age. These skills include the ability to define your job objective based on self-assessment and a knowledge of the world of work, the ability to research, identify, and target potential employers, and the ability to successfully market yourself to those employers you have identified.

Imperative #4:

Attitude. Another crucial factor in job hunting is your attitude. A positive attitude is a must. It shows that you are confident of yourself and what you can do for an employer. This positive, confident attitude comes from knowing who you are and what you want to do, having the information you need, and knowing how to conduct an effective job search.

Reading this book will help you to gain more control of your career direction and job hunt, but much of what you read must be seasoned with practice in order to be of lasting value to you. Such practice activities, or Action Steps as we will call them, will be suggested throughout this book. Sometimes the Action Steps will be for individuals, for those of you who are looking for work on your own. Other times the Action Steps will be for those of you who may either be part of a job hunters' group or who might be interested in forming a small group of people who, like you, are also trying to define their career goals more clearly and search for the job they would most like to have. See pp. 81–82 for additional information on support groups.

Fortunately, the skills of career planning and job-hunting, like riding a bicycle or knowing how to swim, are skills that need only be learned well once in order to be used successfully for a lifetime.

CHAPTER *2:*

Career Planning and Goal Setting

Blue and Gold, 1904

THE CAREER-LIFE PLANNING PROCESS

Because work will consume a large part of your life, planning your career is obviously important. Yet some people give more thought to planning weekend activities than they do to systematically planning their careers. Planning your career means an investment of time and effort. The career planning process involves: 1) gathering and organizing information about yourself and the world of work, 2) establishing your immediate and long-term career objectives, and 3) achieving those objectives through effective job hunting.

The three steps of the career-life planning process form an interdependent cycle. Each step is closely related to the others. In the cycle, the best place to begin is with you. Progress in any of the three steps will enable you to strengthen your understanding of the other steps. For example, when you begin contacting potential employers in the job-hunting step, you will obtain information that will allow you to further clarify your career goals and sharpen your focus.

The Career Decision Making Process

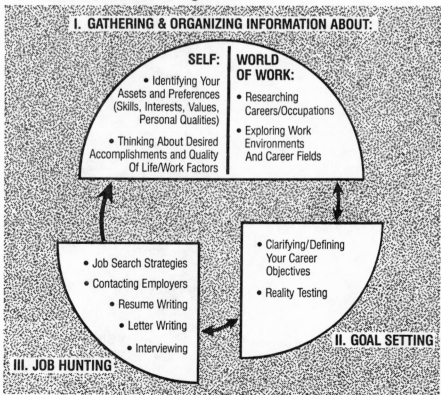

WHERE ARE YOU IN YOUR CAREER PLANNING/JOB SEARCH?

The following checklist is designed to help you determine where you might need help in your career planning and job search activities. The way you answer the questions may yield some important clues for you about your effectiveness in these activities.

Answer each question "yes" or "no," tally your responses and compare your total score to the general guidelines given at the end of the survey.

I. WHAT YOU KNOW ABOUT YOURSELF (self-analysis/assessment)

_____ 1. Can you clearly state what you have gained or want to gain from your education?

_____ 2. Can you explain why you chose (or are thinking about choosing) your major?

_____ 3. Can you name the work activities you do well and most enjoy? How about non-work activities?

_____ 4. Can you list at least five marketable skills and abilities you possess?

_____ 5. For each of your most important job-related experiences, can you list:
    a. Five responsibilities you had?
    b. Five things you learned?
    c. Several contributions you made or things you accomplished?

_____ 6. Can you describe your greatest strength? Your greatest weakness?

_____ 7. Have you clearly defined your geographical preferences and limitations?

_____ 8. Have you determined the salary range you will consider?

II. WHAT YOU KNOW ABOUT THE WORLD OF WORK

_____ 9. Can you name at least three fields of employment in which you are interested?

_____ 10. Do you know the type of organization for which you would like to work?

_____ 11. Can you describe the characteristics of the work environment in which you feel you would be happiest and most productive?

_____ 12. Can you name at least five types of employers that might hire a person with your background?

_____ 13. Can you name at least five position titles that might be appropriate to your interests and abilities?

_____ 14. Do you know at least four or five resources to help you find answers to questions 11, 12, and 13 above?

_____ 15. Can you name at least four sources of information that could help you discover potential employers in a particular geographic area?

_____ 16. Have you recently talked to at least three people who are employed in your field of interest with the purpose of learning more about what they do?

III. GOAL SETTING

_____ 17. Can you clearly and confidently state your career goals?

_____ 18. Can you distinguish your more immediate job objectives from your long-range career goals?

IV. JOB HUNTING

_____ 19. Can you name at least five employers whom you plan to contact regarding employment in the near future?

_____ 20. Are you familiar with the organizational structures, services, programs, or products of the employers whom you are planning to contact?

_____ 21. Can you clearly state why you are interested in working for each employer whom you contact?

_____ 22. Have you prepared a resume with which you are satisfied? Have you asked anyone to critique your resume?

_____ 23. Do you know the questions employers are likely to ask you in an interview?

_____ 24. Have you used any of the following methods to prepare for interviews?
    a. Interview workshops?
    b. Role-playing with a friend or relative?
    c. Role-playing by yourself in front of a mirror?

_____ 25. Do you know ways of developing job leads other than advertised listings?

_____ 26. Have you consulted the schedule of employers who conduct on-campus recruiting visits to determine the organizations with which you might interview?

Add up your "yes" answers for each section and enter them below:

Section I   SELF ANALYSIS/ASSESSMENT   _____

Section II   KNOWLEDGE OF WORK   _____

Section III   GOAL SETTING   _____

Section IV   JOB HUNTING   _____

               TOTAL SCORE   _____

Score 18–26   Excellent! The rest of this book might provide some additional help.

Score 10–17   Good! The rest of this book would certainly be of value.

Score 0–9   Fair. Definitely read on.

Don't be discouraged if you scored low on this "test." Most college students score very low on these questions. Read on and you will no doubt dramatically improve your score.

SELF ASSESSMENT

Any career planning or effective job hunting should begin with self assessment. Many individuals find such analysis difficult or believe it to be fruitless, and therefore are prone to avoid it. "Don't bother me with the details, just tell me where the jobs are" is not an untypical response. Avoiding this step can be a mistake, however, since it serves as the base from which you work. Self assessment will assist you in identifying *suitable* employment opportunities and increase the likelihood of your being satisfied with the job you select. You need to look inward before you look outward. Take time to reflect upon what you can contribute as well as what you want out of work and a career. If you don't know who you are, you cannot market yourself effectively. There will be six questions we will address in this unit that will help you to shape a tentative career objective. The rest of the career planning process will go much more smoothly for you if you make an honest effort to answer these questions. The questions are:

☐ What do you have to offer in terms of the areas of knowledge, abilities, skills, and interests developed through your education and life/ work experience (including volunteer, internship, part-time, and summer work and classroom projects, hobbies, and extracurricular activities)?

☐ What do you want to accomplish through your work?

☐ What are the characteristics of your preferred work environment?

☐ What are your preferred geographical locations?

☐ What is your desired starting salary? What kind of advancement and salary progression would you like to see?

☐ What relationships do you want between your work life and your personal life?

These are questions that may not be easy to answer but yet are important to think about. Throughout the remainder of this chapter, suggestions and activities will be offered that can be of assistance in obtaining answers to these questions and helping you to establish a tentative career objective. Later you will be evaluating this objective against the practicalities and possibilities of appropriate opportunities in the world of work.

What You Have to Offer an Employer

What you have to offer an employer includes your areas of special knowledge, skills and abilities, and personal qualities such as energy, drive and motivation that make you a valuable employee. These attributes will tend to initially define what you would like to do in your work. Foremost are those skills which you have developed and enjoy using.

TYPES OF SKILLS

The skills you have can generally be divided into three groups, as categorized by Sidney Fine: functional, adaptive, and work content skills.

Functional skills, or transferable skills, are more general. They reflect talents and aptitudes, both natural and developed, and include such broad skill areas as: managing, organizing, coordinating, mechanical aptitude, writing, and analyzing. These skills, while maybe developed in a specific context and time frame, are nonetheless transferable to a variety of other situations.

Adaptive skills are developed from life experiences, oftentimes early life experiences, and include such personal qualities or traits as: flexibility, leadership, patience, responsibility, self-reliance, maturity, decisiveness, and independence. These skills are marketable too—do not underestimate them!

Work content skills are developed for specific positions. These skills can be obtained in a wide variety of activities such as: a training program, part-time or summer jobs, internships, or volunteer work. Examples in this category would include: computer programming, typing, welding, and carpentry.

Job hunters tend to place too much emphasis on work content skills and ignore functional and adaptive skills. Content skills require specific training whereas functional and adaptive skills are usually developed out of life experiences. Consequently, the latter skills are easily undervalued because they were developed more easily. Natural talents usually fall into this category as well.

Several studies conducted by Far West Laboratory* have supported the importance of functional and adaptive skills in obtaining employment. In one study, fifty-four percent of the companies surveyed reported that the critical difference between those who get hired and those who do not are adaptive skills such as commitment, interest, initiative, fitting in, assertiveness, enthusiasm, and intelligence. Functional skills such as communication, interpersonal skills, meeting deadlines, and ability to answer questions ranked as being the crucial difference for thirty-eight percent of the companies.

The top ten functional and adaptive non-technical skills named by 48 employers were:

FUNCTIONAL SKILLS		ADAPTIVE SKILLS	
Communication	28	Tactful	21
Writing	28	Assertive	11
Verbal skills	23	Outgoing	9
Interpersonal skills	24	Fast learner	9
Problem solving	15	Positive attitude	8
Analysis	13	Interested in work	8
Listening	10	Good appearance	8
Math skills	10	Motivated	8
Organizing information	10	Self-promoting	8
Research	9	Good self-presentation	8

To see how functional and adaptive skills developed as a student can be transferred to the duties and responsibilities of a career position, carefully review the following diagram.

Following are several activities for assisting you in identifying your own full range of skills.

*C. Murphy and L. Jencks, "Getting a Job—What Skills Are Needed?" A Research Brief; Far West Laboratory, San Francisco.

Transferring Your Skills and Personal Qualities to a Career Job

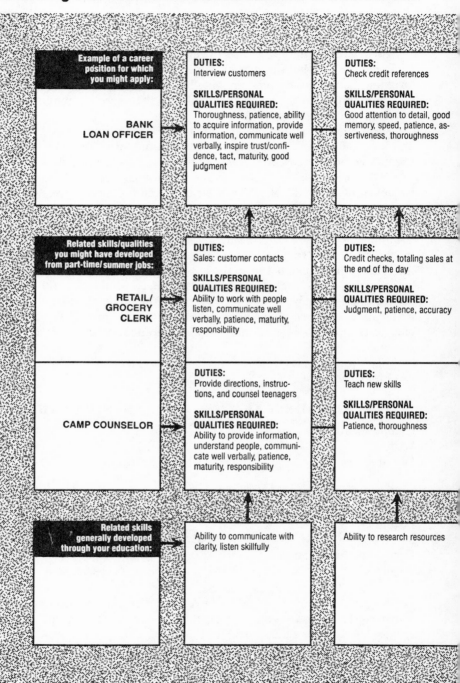

Example of a career position for which you might apply:

BANK LOAN OFFICER

DUTIES:
Interview customers

SKILLS/PERSONAL QUALITIES REQUIRED:
Thoroughness, patience, ability to acquire information, provide information, communicate well verbally, inspire trust/confidence, tact, maturity, good judgment

DUTIES:
Check credit references

SKILLS/PERSONAL QUALITIES REQUIRED:
Good attention to detail, good memory, speed, patience, assertiveness, thoroughness

Related skills/qualities you might have developed from part-time/summer jobs:

RETAIL/ GROCERY CLERK

DUTIES:
Sales: customer contacts

SKILLS/PERSONAL QUALITIES REQUIRED:
Ability to work with people, listen, communicate well verbally, patience, maturity, responsibility

DUTIES:
Credit checks, totaling sales at the end of the day

SKILLS/PERSONAL QUALITIES REQUIRED:
Judgment, patience, accuracy

CAMP COUNSELOR

DUTIES:
Provide directions, instructions, and counsel teenagers

SKILLS/PERSONAL QUALITIES REQUIRED:
Ability to provide information, understand people, communicate well verbally, patience, maturity, responsibility

DUTIES:
Teach new skills

SKILLS/PERSONAL QUALITIES REQUIRED:
Patience, thoroughness

Related skills generally developed through your education:

Ability to communicate with clarity, listen skillfully

Ability to research resources

DUTIES: Decide whether to grant or decline loan, determine level of loan **SKILLS/PERSONAL QUALITIES REQUIRED:** Ability to read, analyze, and evaluate financial statements, good judgment, decisiveness, diplomacy, ability to handle pressure	**DUTIES:** Set up terms of loan: rates, collateral, repayment schedules (deal with large sums of money and confidential information) **SKILLS/PERSONAL QUALITIES REQUIRED:** Facility with detail/figures, ability to deal with complex transactions, good memory, accuracy, honesty, integrity, creativity	**DUTIES:** Present loan package to committee for approval, develop new prospects for loans/other banking services (e.g., trust department) **SKILLS/PERSONAL QUALITIES REQUIRED:** Sales ability, ability to write and speak effectively, interest in current business conditions (interest rates, etc.)
DUTIES: Handle customer complaints and heavy traffic, supervise part-time employees **SKILLS/PERSONAL QUALITIES REQUIRED:** Ability to deal with difficult people and situations, good judgment/decision-making skills	**DUTIES:** Bookkeeping, planning work schedules, cashiering **SKILLS/PERSONAL QUALITIES REQUIRED:** Accuracy, organizational skills, facility with figures/detail	**DUTIES:** Selling, preparing displays **SKILLS/PERSONAL QUALITIES REQUIRED:** Sales ability, ability to speak effectively
DUTIES: Solve disciplinary problems, supervise campers **SKILLS/PERSONAL QUALITIES REQUIRED:** Ability to handle difficult people/situations, good judgment/decision-making skills	**DUTIES:** Developing new plans, coordinating activities and schedules **SKILLS/PERSONAL QUALITIES REQUIRED:** Ability to be creative, plan/organize	**DUTIES:** Promoting activity **SKILLS/PERSONAL QUALITIES REQUIRED:** Sales ability, ability to speak effectively
Interpreting complex material, analyzing/evaluating information, establishing priorities for completing assignments	Summarizing and reporting accurately, basic mathematical skills	Analyzing and evaluating information, cogently expressing a position orally and in writing

| **Action Step** | **IDENTIFYING SKILLS AND ABILITIES.** |

INDIVIDUAL ACTION: One way to get started identifying skills and abilities that will be relevant to your job search is to systematically list such skills. Think about what you do well. Make a list of those abilities you possess without regard to their marketability. Consider those things at which you naturally excel along with those things you have been taught or trained to do. Think about those skills you enjoy using. Identify from your list those skills which you most enjoy using and which you feel are your strongest.

GROUP ACTION: If you have difficulty describing your skills, ask several individuals who know you well to help you. Ask a friend to describe you to an imaginary employer. What do you hear about yourself? Begin making a list of those skills. Try to remember times when you were praised for a task well done. Note, too, any areas of special knowledge you might have.

| **Action Step** | **EXTRACTING YOUR SKILLS FROM YOUR EXPERIENCE.** |

Work content, transferable, and adaptive skills can be identified from a wide range of your activities and experiences. Describe in detail five experiences or accomplishments which you feel provided you an opportunity to show what you can do. These experiences might have happened in a paid part-time or summer job, while doing volunteer work, or while involved in an academic project or extracurricular activity. Here are some sample experiences to show the possibilities you might consider.

Volunteer Work—I advised freshmen and sophomores in college about their general education requirements and some of the planning involved in choosing their majors. I helped them get through the system's bureaucracy by acting as a liaison and referral person in problems with faculty, departments, and school staff, including administrators. I also explained and clarified the college's rules and regulations to the students so that they became less hassled and better able to work with or around them.

Academic Project—For my political science project I studied Oakland's upper middle and upper classes' awareness of and position on current political issues. This involved developing a questionnaire, surveying individuals at their homes, compiling responses, drawing conclusions, and preparing a final report.

Extracurricular Activity—One of the most exciting college activities that I was involved in was the organization of "Homecoming Week." As chairperson of that week, I had the opportunity to work with a variety of people, and to coordinate a diverse range of programs. These included: production of a concert, publication of a magazine for campus-wide distribution, sponsorship of the national frisbee contest, and the introduction of a new activity in which materials were provided to the student body for a craft-making day.

INDIVIDUAL ACTION: Underline the skills found in the experiences you just described. Again check those skills which you most enjoy using and which you feel are your strongest.

GROUP ACTION: Read experiences aloud to each other. Help each other extract the skills which are both explicit and implicit in the experiences.

Use the following lists of functional skills and adaptive skills to stimulate your thinking and to broaden your skills vocabulary.

EXAMPLES OF FUNCTIONAL SKILLS

Researching
Investigating
Analyzing
Questioning
Comparing
Conceptualizing
Classifying
Systematizing
Summarizing
Evaluating
Observing
Perceiving
Reasoning
Assessing
Appraising
Anticipating/Forecasting
Synthesizing

Promoting
Proposing
Persuading
Influencing
Politicking
Motivating
Mediating

Presenting
Public Speaking
Writing
Editing
Translating
Reporting
Interpreting
Teaching
Coaching
Training
Leading Discussions
Explaining
Performing
Entertaining

Planning
Arranging
Organizing
Coordinating
Delegating
Managing
Attending to Detail
Monitoring
Troubleshooting
Initiating

Deciding
Effecting Change
Expediting
Recommending

Designing
Visualizing
Imagining
Drawing
Constructing
Expressing
Conversing
Advising
Counseling
Listening

Empathizing
Serving/Helping
Relating Well to Others
Collaborating
Implementing

Accounting
Calculating
Computing
Budgeting
Measuring
Keeping Records
Problem-Solving
Operating
Repairing

EXAMPLES OF ADAPTIVE SKILLS

Energetic
Punctual
Dependable
Responsible
Enthusiastic
Congenial
Serious
Conscientious
Thoughtful
Perceptive
Efficient
Industrious
Sensitive
Honest
Cheerful
Athletic
Organized
Persuasive
Curious
Discreet
Artistic
Expressive
Analytical

Patient
Sincere
Reliable
Versatile
Loyal
Imaginative
Creative
Calm
Open-minded
Cool-headed
Tactful
Diplomatic
Cooperative
Confident
Humorous
Trustworthy
Economical
Poised
Perseverant
Accurate
Inventive
Observant

We will now integrate the Action Steps just completed into a comprehensive activity.

Take each skill you have identified from the previous Action Steps and transfer them one at a time to the following chart. For each skill, reflect back on experiences in which you have successfully used that particular skill. Then, rank your enjoyment level and your performance level in this skill area. Fill in each column before listing the next skill.

The final summary of the previous skill identification activities is a list specifically tailored for you by you.

SKILL AREAS	ENJOYMENT LEVEL in this skill area					PERFORMANCE LEVEL in this skill area				
	High				Low	High				Low
	5	4	3	2	1	5	4	3	2	1
1.										
2.										
3.										
4.										
5.										
6.										
7.										
8.										
9.										
10.										
11.										
12.										
13.										
14.										
15.										
16.										
17.										
18.										
19.										
20.										

Action Step SKILLS SUMMARY.
When you have completed filling in the Skill Areas chart, the last Action Step, review your rankings of your enjoyment and performance levels and make a prioritized list of the ten skills with the highest combined rankings. Add the top five to the summary sheet at the end of this unit. These are the skills which are likely to play the most important part in your future work.

1) _____

2) _____

3) _____

4) _____

5) _____

6) _____

7) _____

8) _____

9) _____

10) _____

What You Want to Accomplish

Now that you have an idea of what you are capable of doing, you need to decide how you want to apply your skills, abilities and personal qualities. What is the purpose to which you want to direct yourself? What do you most want to do with your life and your career? What do you want to accomplish given your interests and values, as well as the skills you have just identified? Deciding what you WANT to do with what you are CAPABLE of doing will further sharpen your career focus. Concentrate on those activities that have brought you the most enjoyment in your life to date, and try to determine what it was about the activities that made them rewarding. Chances are that you will enjoy similar experiences in the future. Focus on interests and values and try not to connect these to occupational titles at this stage! Identifying occupations before you have finished your self assessment and research of the world of work is premature and will likely result in your excluding a variety of possible career choices.

| **Action Step** | INTEREST CHECKLIST.

The following activities/subjects are of interest to many people. Circle any which interest you. Do not worry about whether or not there seems to be any direct connection to an employment opportunity. The list is not exhaustive, so use your imagination and be sure to add any interest you have which is not listed.

Drawing
Gardening/Horticulture
Tennis
Bird-watching
Construction
Research
Education
Travel
Camping
Photography
Religion
Counseling
Health Planning
Drug Abuse/Alcoholism Treatment
Rehabilitation
Foreign Languages
Consumer Advocacy
Administration
Climbing
City Planning
Animals
Automobiles
Mathematics
Finance
Books
Machines
Television
Human Rights
Investments
Landscaping
Scuba diving
Aviation
Real Estate

Criminal Justice/Corrections
Cooking
Health Care
Writing
Design
Politics
Carpentry
Music
Dance
Selling
World Hunger
Architecture
Transportation
Yoga
Environmental Issues
Computers
Sewing
Law
International Affairs
Labor-Employee Relations
Insects
Stamp Collecting
Stereophonic Equipment
Back-packing
Driving
Theater
Aerospace
Energy
Sports
History
Military Affairs
Science
Others:

You no doubt have discovered that you have more than one interest. Review those you have circled and develop a prioritized list of those interests which, if possible, you would like to directly connect to your work. Add your top five interests in the space below and to the summary sheet at the end of this chapter on pages 36–37.

1) _____

2) _____

3) _____

4) _____

5) _____

Another important aspect of your future work is the intrinsic values associated with that type of employment activity. Following is an activity which will help you decide which work values are most important to you.

| Action Step | WORK REWARDS CHECKLIST.*
Rate each of the following work rewards as they relate to you. Use a scale of one to four with "1" indicating "not at all important" to you and "4" indicating "very important" to you in considering a career. *Prioritize* these variables and then add them to the summary sheet at the end of this unit.

_____ HELP SOCIETY: Do something to contribute to the betterment of the world I live in.

_____ HELP OTHERS: Be involved in helping other people in a direct way, either individually or in small groups.

_____ MAKE DECISIONS: Have the power to decide courses of action, policies, etc.

_____ POWER AND AUTHORITY: Control the work activities or (partially) the destinies of other people.

_____ INFLUENCE PEOPLE: Be in a position to change attitudes or opinions of other people.

_____ KNOWLEDGE: Engage myself in the pursuit of knowledge, truth, and understanding.

*Adapted from *Path: A Career Workbook for Liberal Arts Students*, by Howard Figler, Second Edition, 1979. Cranston, RI: The Carroll Press.

_____ INTELLECTUAL STATUS: Be regarded as a person of high intellectual prowess or as one who is an acknowledged "expert" in a given field.

_____ ARTISTIC CREATIVITY: Engage in creative work in any of several art forms.

_____ CREATIVITY (general): Create new ideas, programs, products, organizational structures, or anything else not following a format previously developed by others.

_____ AESTHETICS: Be involved in studying or appreciating the beauty of things, ideas, etc.

_____ SUPERVISION: Have a job in which I am directly responsible for the work done by others.

_____ RECOGNITION: Be recognized for the quality of my work in some visible or public way.

_____ EXCITEMENT: Experience a high degree of (or frequent) excitement in the course of my work.

_____ ADVENTURE: Have work duties which involve frequent risk-taking.

_____ PROFIT, GAIN: Have a strong likelihood of accumulating large amounts of money or other material gain.

_____ MORAL FULFILLMENT: Feel that my work is contributing significantly to a set of moral standards which I feel are very important.

_____ PHYSICAL CHALLENGE: Have a job that makes physical demands which I would find rewarding.

Another way of approaching the question of the rewards you seek and what it is that you want to accomplish through your work in the future is to project yourself forty or fifty years from now and look at your work life in the past tense. The following action step may provide some help with this.

Action Step   VISUALIZING YOUR FUTURE.
Assume absolutely ideal conditions. *Dare to dream.* This is the best of all possible worlds and you know that you can in fact achieve absolutely anything you would like to achieve. Project yourself into the future to the year 2035. You have just died after a full and happy life. Write down your own obituary as you would like it to appear in your favorite newspaper. Talk about what you have accomplished in terms of 1) productive, enjoyable work; 2) the special knowledge, skills, and abilities you developed over the years; 3) your family life and anything else that it would be important for people to remember you for. Be creative and fantasize to your heart's content.

If writing your obituary does not appeal to you, fantasize that you have been named Person of the Year 2035. Write a news article explaining why, again mentioning 1, 2, and 3 above.

SAMPLE OBITUARY

Barbara Wagner, former editor of Vogue *Magazine, died Sunday at the age of 80 in Columbia Hospital in New York City after a brief illness.*

Prior to her resignation in 2020, she had been with the magazine for fifteen years. Fashion coordinator and former model, Wagner had been on the "Ten Best Dressed Women" list several times during the peak of her career with Vogue.

Born in Huntington, New York, Wagner was a graduate cum laude from Boston University and received her Master's Degree in Journalism from Columbia University.

Before becoming editor of Vogue, *she worked for a small publishing firm of art magazines in Washington, D.C., and as the assistant art and fashion editor for* The New York Times.

She was also a top model for a few years after college and wrote and published several fashion articles which eventually led to her position as editor of Vogue.

Known world-wide as a talented journalist, Wagner also had the prestige and reputation of a fashion and art critic. She was an avid lover of the theater and museums and was a member of the Lincoln and Kennedy Center Performing Arts Series.

She is survived by her husband, Michael, of 2850 5th Avenue, New York, four children and ten grandchildren.

Characteristics of Your Preferred Work Environment

You have identified your skills. You have specified your interest areas and work values in different Action Steps and, as a result, developed some ideas of what you would like to accomplish through your work. Now you are ready to consider characteristics of the work environment that are important to you. You will want to choose a work setting that meshes as much as possible with your own values and personality. Organizations vary according to the type of product or service they provide, organizational style and size, rate of growth, and the physical environment of the workplace. Below are descriptions of items to consider under each of these categories, followed by a partial list of employer types. Use these to establish your criteria for identifying your "ideal" work environment, one that would meet your needs and is conducive to your "style" of working.

Product or Service Provided

Generally, employers fall into two main categories: manufacturing and services. Manufacturing organizations produce and sell tangible products such as electronic equipment, chemicals, building materials, motor vehicles, etc. Service organizations provide services such as education, social services, consulting, insurance, or tax counseling. Some people prefer working with more tangible products, while others prefer working with less tangible things such as services. Beyond this distinction, you will want to consider the types of products or services with which you would like to be associated. Use the lists on pages 22 and 30 to stimulate your thinking.

Organizational Style

Another important factor to consider when choosing an employer is the style or pervading atmosphere in the organization. Some job seekers are more comfortable and productive in an atmosphere characterized by informality in terms of dress, interaction between junior and senior managers, supervision, and work-hour flexibility. Other job seekers prefer a more formal or structured work environment, while still others prefer a combination of styles.

Organization Size

In recent years the trend towards business mergers has created some huge conglomerates. Although there are exceptions, larger, more established organizations offer greater long-term security and a more developed training program than do new businesses. On the other hand, smaller organizations provide more independence, greater variety in work responsibilities and earlier involvement in decision making. Similarly, in an educational institution you might choose to work in a large university where the president remains remote and inaccessible or in a small college where the president is known on a first-name basis. The former may offer greater opportunity for variety; the latter greater opportunity for involvement. Since the majority of businesses are small in size, and the predictions are that the largest number of new jobs will be provided by small organizations, you should not overlook opportunities they offer. Both large and small organizations have advantages and disadvantages for the individual. You need to consider which is best suited to helping you reach your own long-term career goals.

Rate of Growth

How fast or slowly an organization is growing will have a significant effect on all positions within that organization. Faster growing companies and organizations can be exciting and provide many opportunities for speedy advancement. To some workers such an environment may seem dynamic, to other workers, it may seem chaotic. Once again, such a variable is a matter of "fit" with your individual work style and expectations.

Physical Environment of the Workplace

You should also consider the physical environment in which you would most like to be working. Would you like to work in an urban, suburban, or rural setting? Indoors or outdoors? Would you like to travel? Would you like to remain in an office? Would you like a formal setting with an opportunity to wear fashionable clothes or a more relaxed environment with an opportunity to wear jeans? The following Action Steps can help to more clearly identify your preferred work environment and to translate your work environment preferences to specific employer possibilities.

| Action Step | PREFERRED WORK ENVIRONMENT CHARACTERISTICS.*

INDIVIDUAL ACTION: Listed below are some sample factors which relate to work environment characteristics. Use a scale of one to four to rate these characteristics with "1" indicating "not at all important" to you and "4" indicating "very important" to you in considering a career.

_____ PUBLIC CONTACT: Have a great deal of day-to-day contact with people.

_____ WORK WITH OTHERS: Have close working relationships with a group; work as a team toward common goals.

_____ AFFILIATION: Be recognized as a member of a particular organization.

_____ FRIENDSHIP: Develop close personal relationships with people as a result of my work activities.

_____ COMPETITION: Engage in activities which pit abilities against others where there are clear win-and-lose outcomes.

_____ WORK UNDER PRESSURE: Work in situations where time pressure is prevalent and/or the quality of my work is judged critically by supervisors, customers, and others.

_____ CHANGE AND VARIETY: Have work responsibilities which frequently change in their content and setting.

_____ PRECISION WORK: Work in situations where there is very little tolerance for error.

_____ STABILITY: Have a work routine and job duties that are largely predictable and not likely to change over a long period of time.

*Adapted from *Path: A Career Workbook for Liberal Arts Students,* by Howard Figler, Second Edition, 1979. Cranston, RI: The Carroll Press.

_____ SECURITY: Be assured of keeping my job and a reasonable financial reward.

_____ FAST PACE: Work in circumstances where there is a high pace of activity, and work must be done rapidly.

_____ LOCATION: Find a place to live (town, geographical area) which is conducive to my lifestyle and affords me the opportunity to do the things I most enjoy.

_____ COMMUNITY: Live in a town or city where I can get involved in community affairs. Or work in a position that involves community activities/affairs.

_____ INDEPENDENCE: Be able to determine the nature of my work without significant direction from others; not have to do what others tell me to do.

_____ TIME FREEDOM: Have work responsibilities which I can work at according to my own time schedule; no specific working hours required.

GROUP ACTION: Conduct a discussion on the variety of factors characterizing work environments. Some suggestions are listed below. Write them on a blank flip chart, then post the list for discussion.

☐ size
☐ public or private sector
☐ educational, non-profit
☐ business and industry
☐ growing or slowing
☐ management philosophy
☐ qualities of the physical environment
☐ training opportunities
☐ nature of the work schedule
☐ content or subject area
☐ union or non-union
☐ outdoors or indoors
☐ rigid hierarchy or loose
☐ policies of company regarding frequent moves, advancement, etc.
☐ benefits
☐ salaries
☐ locally owned or national
☐ branch or franchise
☐ type of product/service
☐ qualities of co-workers
☐ advancement potential

Give members of your group time to discuss the items, then have each person list five characteristics most preferred and five to avoid. Brainstorm as well some typical settings where these characteristics might be found.

PREFERRED   TO BE AVOIDED

1) _____   1) _____

2) _____   2) _____

3) _____   3) _____

4) _____   4) _____

5) _____   5) _____

SETTINGS WHERE PREFERRED CHARACTERISTICS
MIGHT BE FOUND

1) _____

2) _____

3) _____

Once you have defined your preferences, you need to prioritize them according to which are essential in a work environment and which are optional. The following Action Step can help you to make such a ranking.

| Action Step | RANKING WORK ENVIRONMENT
CHARACTERISTICS. From the previous inventories and any other considerations you have made, make a list of no more than ten items which are important to you in the working environment. Then rank these items from most important to least important. Read down the list and ask yourself for each item, "Is this a crucial factor in my accepting a job offer?" or "Do I need this variable in my next position to be happy, effective, and/or successful?" If some item on your list priority should shift from "crucial" to "desirable," draw a line through the list at the point where this shift occurs. All factors above this line are "musts"; all factors below the line are "wants."

Not only will this help you in defining your career objectives, but you now also possess an "objective" resource for double-checking any future job offer you receive. You will be able to compare what the opportunity offers against what you previously decided were necessary characteristics of your work environment.

List your top five preferred work environment characteristics below and then add them to the summary sheet at the end of this chapter on pages 36–37.

1) _____

2) _____

3) _____

4) _____

5) _____

Another important aspect of your working environment is the type of employer in which you are interested. Use the Action Step below to begin identifying your preferences.

| **Action Step** | **EMPLOYER TYPE CHECKLIST.**

Circle all of the employer types listed below in which you might have some interest. At this stage, do not worry about whether or not you are qualified for the jobs you would normally associate with these employer types.

Accounting Firms
Banks
Investment Firms
Hospitals
Business Corporations
State Government
Labor Unions
Trade Associations
Marketing Research Firms
Insurance Companies
Tax Consultants
Research and Development
Management Consulting Firms
Advertising Agencies
Department Stores
Public/Private Schools
Community Organizations
    (YMCA, Scouts, etc.)

Federal Government
Symphony Orchestras
Law Enforcement Agencies
Technical Journals
Botanical Gardens
Utility Companies
Manufacturing Firms
Opera Companies
Mining/Petroleum Firms
Art Galleries
Air, Bus, Rail, and Shipping Lines
Travel Agencies
Magazines, Newspapers
Public Relations Firms
Employment Agencies
Chambers of Commerce
Fund-Raising Organizations
Bookstores

Colleges/Universities
National and State Parks
Publishing Houses
Film Companies
Libraries
Engineering Firms
Youth Organizations
Museums
Radio/TV Industry
Historical Societies
Rehabilitation
Day Care/Child Care
Correctional Institutes
Housing Authorities
City Government
Animal Hospitals
Audio/Visual Firms
City/Town Planners
Camps
Photography Studios
Architecture Firms
Environmental Organizations
Construction Firms
Food Processors
Motor Vehicle Sales/Service

Educational TV/Film
Social Service Agencies
Test Development Corporations
Private Foundations
Import-Export Companies
Regional Planning
Weather Bureaus
Church Organizations
Advocacy/Lobbying Organizations
Research Laboratories
Military Organizations
Data Processing Organizations
Hotel/Motel/Tourism
Nursing Homes
Pharmaceuticals
Political Organizations
Real Estate Firms
Public Opinion Pollsters
Medical Clinics
Aerospace Contractors
Sports Leagues
Communications Companies
Agricultural Firms
Self-Employed/Own Business

Review those employer types that you have circled and again make a prioritized list of those that are most appealing to you, and add them to the summary sheet at the end of this chapter on pages 36–37.

1) _____

2) _____

3) _____

4) _____

5) _____

Additional Factors

To further specify your initial career goal, you should consider three other factors: where you would geographically like to work, how much money you need or would like to earn, and the relationship you would like to have between your work and personal life.

a) Your *geographic location* may be completely open-ended, in which case you are willing to relocate wherever you might be assigned for training or hired for permanent employment. Some job hunters prefer to stay in the area where most of their family lives, others like to explore new regions of the country. Some have strong climate preferences, others want an urban or rural environment. Whatever factors are important to you in deciding where you want to live and work, it is important to note that some industries tend to be concentrated in different areas of the country. This may affect the availability of certain kinds of work in some locations.

| Action Step | **GEOGRAPHICAL PREFERENCES.**

List in order of preference the three geographical areas where you would prefer to live and work. Be as specific as possible, for example, indicate San Francisco, the Bay area, Southwest Florida, Boston, Phoenix rather than the West Coast, the Southeast United States, etc. Such decisions as geographical, urban/rural environment, and climate preferences are, of course, a personal choice that is influenced by many variables, including location of family and friends, employment opportunities, leisure activities/interests, etc.

1) _____

2) _____

3) _____

Add these three locations to the summary sheet at the end of this chapter on pages 36–37.

b) Only you can decide how much *money* you feel you need or would like to earn. It is relatively easy to obtain from the university or college you attend or have attended, current information concerning salary offers made to individuals graduating with your degree or accepting the type of job in which you are interested. Ask for such information at your campus career planning and placement center. Many students use such statistics to determine the "market rate" they should request or expect from an employer. Besides your starting salary there are two other factors you should consider as you attempt to answer this question. The first is the importance to you of longer term earning potential and the second is the importance of job security. The following Action Step outlines an approach to computing your basic financial needs.

Action Step CALCULATING YOUR FINANCIAL NEEDS.
One approach for determining the salary you need or should expect involves determining your financial needs based upon the lifestyle you are accustomed to or expect to live. Calculate a budget of such a lifestyle by tracking your current spending habits. Start with those expenses which are fixed such as housing, car, and insurance payments and then add your variable expenses such as food, entertainment, and travel. Once you have a base to work from you can begin to estimate additional expenses which are likely to accrue after you are employed, such as repayment of student loans, investment in work clothing, and the additional costs involved in raising your standard of living. Also consider the cost of living in the geographical area where you intend to live, adjusting your figures accordingly.

SAMPLE MONTHLY BUDGET

Rent	$ _____
Utilities	$ _____
Other Household Expenses (furnishings etc.)	$ _____
Car Payments	$ _____
Car Insurance	$ _____
Car Expenses (gas etc.)	$ _____
Student Loan Payment	$ _____
Food	$ _____
Entertainment	$ _____
Travel	$ _____
Clothes	$ _____
Other Insurance	$ _____
Gifts/Contributions	$ _____
Savings	$ _____
Other: Total	$ _____

This systematic analysis will determine a salary figure (not accounting for income tax) that you can confidently feel is an accurate estimate of your basic financial needs. The low end of your expected salary range should be the minimum you would be willing to accept (your basic survival salary) no matter how good the job looks; the high end should be the highest amount you realistically can hope to be making in your first or next job, based on your research. Enter this salary range here and on the summary sheet at the end of this chapter on page 36–37.

Salary Range:

—

(low end)   (high end)

c) The *relationship between work and your personal life* is another issue that only you can decide. Many people have a strong preference to limit the amount of hours they work and keep their work and personal lives separate, while others do not mind bringing work home, both physically and mentally. For most, this issue is largely a question of time. How much time do you want to devote to your work and how much time do you want to pursue other things that may be important in your life, such as social relationships, family, recreational or cultural activities? Jobs vary dramatically in their time demands and you should be aware of any conflicts in this area with your own preferred lifestyle.

While many people, especially early in their careers, are willing to sacrifice personal time for their jobs, working extra hours will not necessarily bring you greater organizational rewards. Rewards are usually linked to what you achieve for the organization, not the number of extra hours you spend or how busy you appear to be.

Action Step A TIME ANALYSIS OF PERSONAL AND PROFESSIONAL GOALS. Try to determine the number of hours you spend a week on personal activities including life maintenance activities like grocery shopping, laundry, etc., as well as on hobbies, cultural activities, recreation, and other interests. Estimate the amount of time a week you spend, or expect to spend, with personal friends and significant others. Estimate the amount of time the job/career you seek will likely require. How demanding will your time commitments be? Which aspects of your anticipated schedule are most important to you and which can be flexible, if necessary? Discuss potential time conflicts with those people who may be affected in your personal life. How does it all add up? How can you achieve the balance you prefer? Summarize the balance you hope to achieve and include this on the summary sheet at the end of this chapter on pages 36–37.

GOAL SETTING

You should now have enough information to establish a career goal (your general direction) and an immediate job objective (the more specific statement of your overall career goal). Your objective should integrate your priorities as you have determined them from the exercises in this chapter. It will represent a combination of all those factors you have identified as being important to you. Be prepared for the need to possibly compromise on some of the factors as a result of conflict between your responses. Your objective should be as specific as possible without overly limiting opportunities you wish to consider (a sometimes difficult task to achieve). For example, "An entry-level position in public relations for a medium-sized, private company which involves client contact," would be better than, "A position working with people in public relations." Or, "Using my written and oral communication skills, organizational ability, and leadership qualities to organize community support for improved zoning ordinances in Santa Clara County" would be better than "Entry-level position in a community action organization."

Although it is just an initial decision as to what you think you want and would be happy doing for a career, it is an important step to make in the career planning process. Your objective will serve as your starting point for researching the world of work as explained in Chapter Three. After your research, you should have an even sharper focus on your career objective. Then, having decided what you are looking for, you can begin in earnest to look for it. Chapter Four will cover in detail the art and science of job hunting. The following pages will help you to summarize your progress so far.

Action Step CAREER/LIFE PLANNING SUMMARY SHEET. Use the following career chart to list in priority order within each category those elements important to you in your career.

Sample Career/Life Planning Summary Sheet

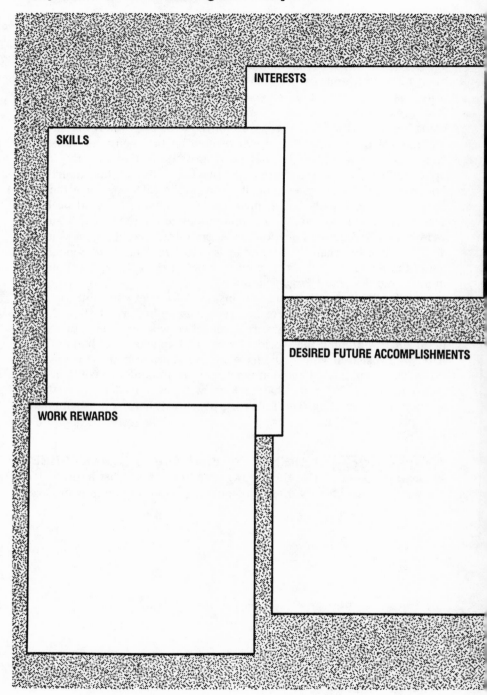

INTERESTS

SKILLS

DESIRED FUTURE ACCOMPLISHMENTS

WORK REWARDS

[To be filled in as basis for objective stated on p. 62]

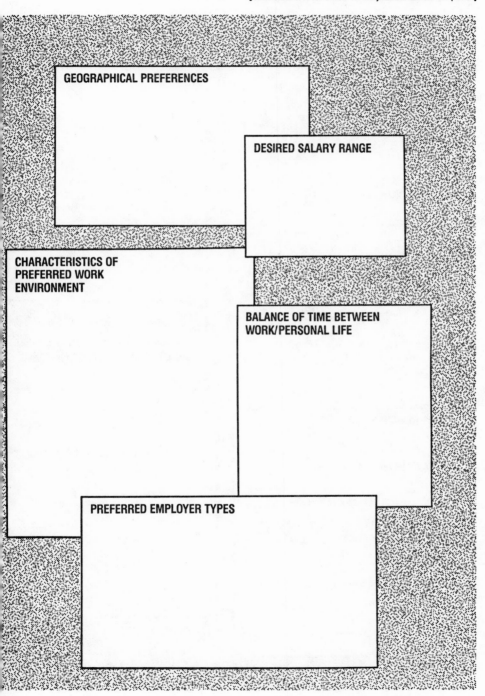

GEOGRAPHICAL PREFERENCES

DESIRED SALARY RANGE

CHARACTERISTICS OF PREFERRED WORK ENVIRONMENT

BALANCE OF TIME BETWEEN WORK/PERSONAL LIFE

PREFERRED EMPLOYER TYPES

Sample Career/Life Planning Summary Sheet

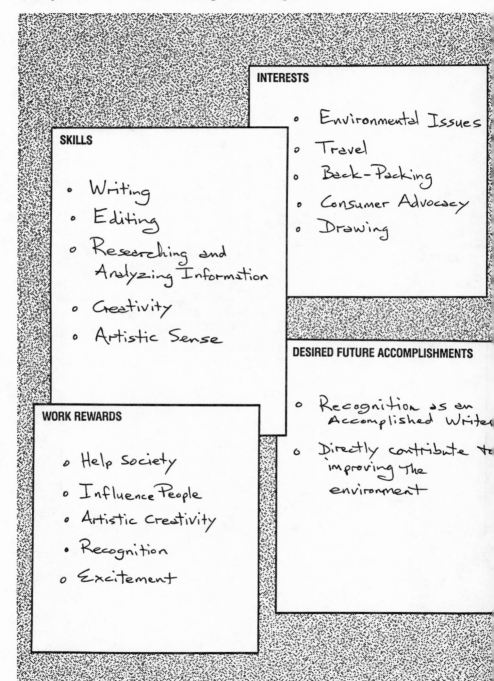

INTERESTS

- Environmental Issues
- Travel
- Back-Packing
- Consumer Advocacy
- Drawing

SKILLS

- Writing
- Editing
- Researching and Analyzing Information
- Creativity
- Artistic Sense

DESIRED FUTURE ACCOMPLISHMENTS

- Recognition as an Accomplished Writer
- Directly contribute to improving the environment

WORK REWARDS

- Help Society
- Influence People
- Artistic Creativity
- Recognition
- Excitement

GEOGRAPHICAL PREFERENCES

- Washington, D.C.
- San Francisco, CA
- Atlanta, GA

DESIRED SALARY RANGE

$14,000 — $20,000

CHARACTERISTICS OF PREFERRED WORK ENVIRONMENT

- Small-Medium Sized
- Informal Atmosphere
- Public or Non-Profit
- Issue-Oriented
- Independence

BALANCE OF TIME BETWEEN WORK/PERSONAL LIFE

- Enough time for friends
- Time for tennis once a week and concerts twice a month
- Maximum 50-Hour Work Week

PREFERRED EMPLOYER TYPES

- National Lobbying Organization
- Governmental Agency
- Publishing House

| Action Step | STATING YOUR CAREER OBJECTIVES.

INDIVIDUAL ACTION: Develop your career objective by weaving together the key elements you identified on the Career Planning Summary Sheet. For example:

> I would like to use my proven writing ability, editorial experience, ability to research information, creativity, artistic sense and genuine interest in and concern for the environment working as a writer/ editor for a publication produced by a national organization promoting environmental concern, with offices in Washington, D.C. I want to be in a position where I can influence people and gain personal recognition for my work. I want to be making $14,000–$20,000 per year and work no more than 50 hours per week, leaving time to socialize with friends, attend concerts at least twice a month, and play tennis once a week.

GROUP ACTION: Once you have developed on your own the statement of your career objectives, review it with the members of your group. Ask for reactions, suggestions for improving the wording of your statement, and questions about what you may not have included. Brainstorm with the group other possible ways of combining the elements on your Career Planning Summary Sheet.

CHAPTER *3*:

Finding Out About the World of Work

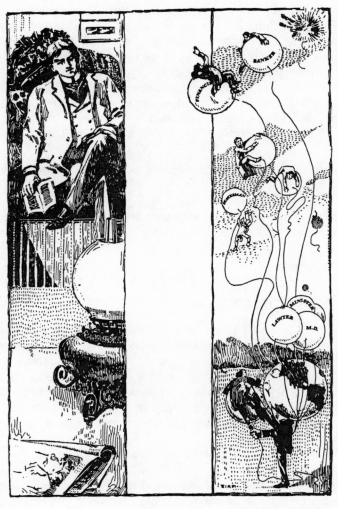

Blue and Gold, 1899

Once you have gathered, analyzed, and organized information about yourself and have tentatively determined your career goals, you need to find out more about that particular kind of work and the range of employment opportunities it offers. Your research into the world of work will not only give you a chance to confirm the feasibility of your tentative career goals, but will also ease you into the task of job hunting. You will be able to use much of the information you collect and many of the contacts that you make at this stage when you start to look for a specific employment opportunity later on.

Information about the world of work can be obtained from four sources:

1) printed resources, such as career pamphlets, occupational guides and some directories;
2) computerized resources;
3) people resources (personal discussions with individuals in your area of career interest); and
4) actual work experience.

PRINTED RESOURCES

Printed information is available about most career fields. In fact you may have a problem in limiting the information you collect to that which is most pertinent to your career objective. Clearly define the category or type of information you are seeking prior to your research. For example, you might initially want to know the types and titles of positions for recent college graduates found in the textiles industry. Or you might want to find out the typical duties and responsibilities of a particular position, or the usual qualifications that are expected.

Many public libraries, and most college libraries, have sections devoted to occupational information and employer directories. If you have access to a career library such as those found in career planning and placement centers on most college and university campuses, you can also refer to employer brochures and annual reports, job market studies, and employment listings as part of your research.

In researching the world of work you need a plan for obtaining information. Initially, your search may seem ambiguous and undefined, but as you learn more about different possibilities you will become more focused. Of course, the self analysis that was done in the previous unit will serve as a great starting point for what you want and need in a job. You need to have a general level of understanding about an industry to be able to ask intelligent questions about careers in that field. By answering the following general questions, more specific questions will be raised in your mind that can be asked of individuals who work in the profession of your interest.

☐ What career fields initially seem compatible with my goals?

☐ What organizations employ people who are interested in these careers?

☐ What do people in these career fields actually do?

☐ What do people like most/least about working in these career fields?

☐ How does one best prepare for these career fields?

Printed occupational information can be consulted to clarify and confirm your initial impressions about the career field and for more detailed occupational descriptions. Among the more widely used general career information references are:

☐ *Encyclopedia of Careers*
☐ *Dictionary of Occupational Titles*
☐ *Occupational Outlook Handbook*
☐ *Occupational Thesaurus*

In addition to these general career references, printed information on specific career fields is usually available free of charge from the national professional organizations representing that career field. Consult the National Trade and Professional Association Directory at your library for names and addresses. Also, several publishers offer books or pamphlets on specific careers as part of "career series" information.

Two examples of such series are the "Opportunities in _____" series published by VGM Career Horizons, Skokie, Ill., and the "Career Options Series for Undergraduate Women" (men can read it too!) published by Catalyst, New York City.

In addition to these formal career publications, don't overlook the value of background information on your career field which you can glean from newspapers, magazines, professional journals and other special interest publications.

Despite the possible drawbacks of printed material being out-dated or not providing a comprehensive description of the work in which you are particularly interested, you must READ before you start going to people for information about your ideal career field. Reading published materials will provide the base of knowledge you need to be well-informed and intelligent as you use other career resources.

| Action Step | EXPLORING YOUR IDEAL CAREER FIELD.
Based on your stated career objective begin identifying and reviewing books, articles and other printed material that will begin to answer your questions about that career field. Start with the library at the career planning and placement center on your campus.

COMPUTERIZED RESOURCES

Computerized resources are gaining in prominence and can provide current information about a wide variety of career fields. These resources are regularly updated and overcome the dated character of many printed career materials. Perhaps the best way to seek information through computerized resources is with the assistance of trained personnel at your library or career planning and placement center. Typical career data bases include a description of duties and responsibilities, qualifications, employment outlook, and salary information. Some computerized career guidance systems offer one or both of the following programs:

1) CAREER DEVELOPMENT PROGRAMS—These programs administer general interest inventories and questions relating to work values and attitudes and then suggest appropriate occupations based on your indicated occupational interests, needs, abilities, values, and goals.

2) OCCUPATIONAL INFORMATION PROGRAMS—These programs provide specific searches for information on occupations. Information is indexed by job duties and responsibilities, entry-level qualifications, pay, location, working conditions, training programs, and related topics.

Depending on the specific system that is available, you can obtain varying degrees of assistance. The following are among the most well-known systems used on college campuses today.

☐ SYSTEM OF INTERACTIVE GUIDANCE AND INFORMATION (SIGI)—One of the most successful programs, this system is used by a number of colleges and universities. The system both helps the student with career decision making and provides occupational information. The program has six parts: Value, Locate, Compare, Prediction, Planning, and Strategy. "Value" helps the student to identify and assign weights to occupational values. "Locate" identifies occupations that meet or exceed the expressed values. "Compare" uses game-like situations to interrelate and test the potential occupations and values. "Prediction," which is tailored for the specific institution, predicts the student's chances of succeeding in the courses that are related to particular occupations. "Planning," which is also tailored, indicates what the student must do to qualify for entrance into a particular career. "Strategy" examines the trade-offs between rewards and risks of specific occupations.

☐ DISCOVER—This program is designed to help the student make career decisions and develop rational strategies for attaining occupational goals. It includes modules on: Clarifying Values, Values and Occupations, Effective Decision Making, Decision Making in Careers, Organization of the Occupational World, Browsing Occupations, Reviewing Interests and Strengths, Making a List of Occupations to Explore, Getting Information About Occupations to Explore, Narrowing a List of Occupations, and Exploring Specific Career Paths.

☐ GUIDANCE INFORMATION SYSTEMS (GIS)—This is a comprehensive career information system designed for use by anyone involved in career planning. It helps the user get information about 850 different primary occupations, sources of financial aid, etc. It contains five national data files and various regional and state files.

☐ COMPUTERIZED VOCATIONAL INFORMATION SYSTEM (CVIS)—Another combined system, CVIS allows the student to enter data on grades, abilities, and interests, etc. as well as levels of training and responsibility desired and categories of interest. Consistency is checked and qualifying occupations are presented by the computer. Information on more than 400 occupations, 1600 universities and colleges, and 170 national and local sources of financial aid is contained in the system.

☐ CHOICES—Developed by a branch of the Canadian government, this system has one of the most extensive occupational listings of the major career placement computer systems (700 primary occupations and 3000 related occupations). After entering data on interests, aptitudes, and occupational information, the computer presents a list of occupations meeting the desired criteria. The student can ask that detailed information on any three occupations be provided for comparison. The system will also identify why any specific occupation is not listed based on occupational characteristics.

☐ CAREER INFORMATION SYSTEM (CIS)—This system, developed in Oregon, is an occupational information system that focuses primarily on in-state rather than national occupational information. It is particularly useful for helping older students who are seeking new careers. It provides information concerning required skills, licenses, education and training and in-state institutions, programs that meet occupational training requirements, pertinent occupational publications, in-state exploratory clubs, and a contact listing of individuals active in prospective occupations. Adaptations of this system have been developed in several states under different names.

Consult a career librarian or career counselor for computer programs specific to the state where you are planning to find work.

Action Step USING COMPUTERIZED RESOURCES. Research additional information on specific career fields which you identified in the last chapter. Try to access the computer systems mentioned in this section and seek help if needed from appropriate library or career planning and placement personnel.

PEOPLE RESOURCES

Another way of collecting information about the type of work in which you are interested is to talk with those who are currently doing or supervising such work. This is a way to build on your research of printed and computerized resources and evaluate your impressions of specific kinds of work in which you have an interest. You can learn how others became qualified for their occupations and positions, what a typical day is like for them, and what skills they feel someone entering the field must possess to get hired. Besides learning more about specific career fields and occupations, researching your ideal career in this way also gives you a chance to know more about specific employers and their work environments.

Talking to people about the career field you are researching is different from job interviewing or from simply asking an employer for a job. It is less formal and often more informative, since neither you nor the person you are talking to is evaluating the discussion for the purpose of making a specific employment decision. Instead, there is an exchange of information that is usually open and candid in an atmosphere that is nonthreatening.

Your purpose is to collect additional information that will assist you in making a career decision. Your requests to talk with people should be based on your genuine need to know more about a career field before you definitely decide what you want to do and where you want to work. This method of research is not a scheme or a trick to get you in the door to talk to a potential employer about a job.

Gathering information from people in the field can help you to overcome career planning obstacles that many individuals encounter:

1. APPLYING YOUR BACKGROUND. Talking to people allows you to learn more about the positions, duties, qualifications, and personality

traits of people in the field of your interest. You can obtain specific job titles and information about career paths. This information will help you to know how you can best apply your background within your field of interest. For example, a sales representative might describe a certain "sales personality" that leads to success within her organization. She could describe how she spends a typical day on her job. She could tell you what her next likely position would be if she succeeds at her job. She could describe the longer range career paths for sales representatives within the organization and how many of the executives previously had sales backgrounds.

2. SUGGESTIONS FOR EXPERIENCE. If you feel you lack relevant experience to get the career position you want, you can ask for specific suggestions on how to acquire such experience. This might include suggestions for additional coursework, internships, part-time positions, etc. In addition, a lack of experience can often be compensated for by knowledge of an organization's structure, services and problems. Having this knowledge will enable you to uncover unmet needs within the organization that you might wish to address with your current skills.

3. KNOWLEDGE OF OPPORTUNITIES. In many fields, few jobs are ever openly advertised, so it is difficult to assess the range of opportunities without talking to people in the field. Unfortunately many students and recent graduates feel that they do not have access to knowledgeable and influential people. Talking to people about the career field you are considering can help you to learn more about opportunities in general and establish professional contacts that can serve as valuable resources for discovering specific opportunities later, after you have definitely decided on your career objective and begun your job search.

Using people resources is especially appropriate if you are still in school, since the activity is very much like a research project. Students may specifically state that they are collecting information to use in deciding among career alternatives. In fact, some students select topics for term papers and research projects that are closely related to their career interests so that they can talk with people in their career field at the same time they are fulfilling an academic requirement.

Those who have not done this before are often concerned that no one will be willing to talk with them, or that they must have a better reason to justify using a busy person's time than to simply ask questions. This is not usually the case, though some misuse of this method by people who were really job hunters and not people trying to meet a genuine need for information has caused some individuals to be less receptive than in the past. Many people enjoy talking about their jobs, especially to students who are interested in the same field. Your success will be directly related to the care that you take in the process.

Arranging a Meeting to Research Your Ideal Career Field

You will want to identify, by name, the person you wish to interview so that you are contacting an individual, not a job title. If you cannot find the name, but know the kind of work in which you are interested, you may call and ask for the name of the person in charge of the section or division that handles the function in which you are interested.

Directories can be used to obtain names of individuals you can contact. They are typically indexed by organizational name, geographical area, products and/or services. Because names and even addresses frequently change, they should be confirmed prior to contacting any individuals. Directories may not include smaller or newer organizations which may be of interest in your information search. You may wish want to augment your research by referring to the yellow pages of the telephone book in your preferred geographical area and then calling the organization to get the name of the person with whom you should be talking.

An extensive listing of general and specific directories for different career fields is located in the appendix of this book. Don't overlook your own personal contacts. People you already know can lead you to people who are working in your field of interest.

Start with people who are "low threat," such as family, friends, alumni, etc. Develop an approach with which you are comfortable and gain experience in areas that are of less importance to you, so that little is lost while you are gaining confidence. Save the people or organizations of greatest interest until you have had some practice.

Use the approach with which you are both comfortable and effective. A standard approach is for you to make an initial contact over the telephone or through a letter. A phone call first will allow you to confirm names and titles of those with whom you are interested in speaking. When you contact the individual over the telephone, introduce yourself, state your purpose and ask for a time to meet to discuss your questions. Ask for twenty or thirty minutes of the person's time—and stick to the length of time agreed upon. If the person is unable to meet with you, you may ask if the person has time to answer some of your questions over the phone. If possible, it is almost always preferable to have one of your own personal contacts arrange an appointment for you. If so, make sure that person clearly understands your purpose for having the meeting. Your telephone skills and introduction can be easily practiced with friends.

If you are uncomfortable or feel you do not come across very well over the phone, or if you choose to do your research out of the vicinity, it may be possible to set up your meetings through correspondence. Sample letters regarding such meetings can be found on pages 51 and 52.

Preparing for Your Meeting

First make a list of the questions you still have unanswered about your potential career field. Your questions should be sincere, not simply made up for the purposes of talking to an employer. They might, for example, try to uncover the differences between two types of positions or two specific companies. Your questions might explore how the person obtained the position currently held and what background and experience was necessary to get the job. You might ask for advice as to how best to enter that specific career field today. No matter what you ask, try to make every conversation a learning experience and you will never be disappointed with the time you spend.

Remember that your purpose is to gather information from someone who is working in an area of interest to you. You are not asking for a job; you are searching for information which will help you to understand the realities of working in that field. You will be guiding the discussion.

Always be respectful of the other person's time. Before leaving ask for suggestions of other people who might have information that would be of value to you. This activity is an opportunity to speak with others who are interested in the same things you are—have fun with it!

SAMPLE QUESTIONS

The following questions can be used as a general guide and adapted to your specific situation as appropriate. A tailored list could even be brought to an interview as an aid in collecting information relevant to your research.

1. What is your job like?
   What do you do in a typical day?
   What kinds of problems do you deal with?
   What kinds of decisions do you make?

2. What are the most important personal satisfactions and dissatisfactions connected with your occupation?

3. What social obligations go along with a job in your occupation?
   Are there organizations you are expected to join?
   Are there other things you are expected to do outside of work hours?

4. What things did you do before you entered this occupation?
   What has been most helpful to you?

5. What sorts of changes are occurring in your occupation?
   What external factors affect this occupation?

6. How does a person progress in your field?
   What is the best way to enter this occupation?
   What are the advancement opportunities?
   What are the major qualifications for success in this particular occupation?

7. Could you suggest any other people who work in this field or in related fields with whom I could talk?

Following up a Meeting

To get the most value out of the time you spend and the contact you made, follow these suggestions:

Record Keeping. Keep good notes on your discussions, either during or immediately following each meeting. Evaluate what you learned and record the names and addresses of any new contacts in an appropriate place. Well kept records will be an asset when you definitely decide what you would like to do and make the transition from an information seeker to job hunter.

Thank-You Notes. Send thank-you letters to each person with whom you talked. A few lines can indicate your appreciation of their time and the value you derived from the meeting. This gesture of old-fashioned courtesy can also help you to be remembered should you contact the individual again in the future.

Periodic Recontact. Being careful not to make a pest of yourself, keep your contacts informed of the progress of your field research and the assistance any of their referrals gave you. If you keep in contact you are more likely to establish an on-going professional relationship. Your interest in them may be reciprocated as they share with you information that is of value or interest to you, including, eventually, potential job openings.

Action Step Use the resources suggested above to develop a list of people to contact who could be helpful to you in researching you career field. Prepare the questions you wish to discuss with them and begin arranging appointment times for meetings with them. Set up your record-keeping system so that you can track your progress.

SAMPLE LETTER REQUESTING AN INFORMATIONAL MEETING

```
                                    111 San Francisco Blvd.
                                    Berkeley, CA 94707
                                    (415) 555-6422
                                    November 17, 1984


Mr. James Monroe, Vice President
Asia Division
Bank International
20 Pine Street
New York, NY    10015

Dear Mr. Monroe:

    Eleanor Smith of your San Francisco subsidiary suggested that
I direct this inquiry to you.  She recommended you as a knowledge-
able person in international banking.

    I will be completing my Master's degree in Asian Studies in
May, 1985.  In this interdisciplinary program, I have emphasized
modern political theory, economics and the language of Japan.

    I will be in New York City from January 4th through the 15th
and would appreciate the opportunity to interview you to gather
first-hand information about careers in international banking and
Bank International.  I will come prepared with specific questions.
Your advice on how best to apply my unique background to this field
would prove very valuable.  If you will not be available, please
forward this request to any of your colleagues.

    Thank you in advance for considering this request.  I will
telephone within two weeks to confirm an appointment.

                            Sincerely,

                            Joan Lacy

                            Joan Lacy
```

SAMPLE THANK-YOU LETTER FOR AN INFORMATIONAL MEETING

1234 Odage Avenue
Berkeley, CA 94708
(415) 555-5556
March 25, 1985

Ms. Sharon Hiyumi
Sales Representative
Apex Chemical Company
San Jose, CA 95125

Dear Ms. Hiyumi:

Thank you for the informative discussion we had yesterday in your office. It was particularly useful to have my questions about the field of chemical sales answered by someone with your experience and training. I appreciated the tour of your facility and the opportunity to see people at work on such a variety of projects.

Our discussion and tour have helped me to clarify my career plans. I am more determined than ever to pursue a sales career. I will be contacting the people whom you suggested.

Thank you again.

Sincerely,

Susan Strom

Susan Strom

A Word About Employment Trends

Many people are influenced in their research of the world of work by so-called "employment trends," forecasts of what industries and professions will be "hot" in the upcoming year or decade. Such information should be used, if at all, with extreme caution for several reasons. Most of the data that is used in such forecasts are based upon very limited examples and time frames. For example, one such study queries only college recruiters, even though many job categories are filled in ways other than through on-campus recruiting efforts. Much of the information is usually collected early in the academic year—prior to most job-hunting activity—to be available for announcement to the media before the end of the year. As a result the data is incomplete and usually only reflects the areas of the very highest job market demand.

Employment trends are rarely categorized by geographic region, so that there may be a high demand for the field of your choice nationwide, but a glut of qualified applicants in the specific area where you would like to live.

If you consider employment trend information, you should check the information specifically with people who are working in the fields of your interest. Do not assume specific forecasts are valid without verifying the information first.

You may have better luck keeping abreast of employment changes by keeping informed of the general activities in the career field in which you are interested. Watch for information in daily newspapers or subscribe to newsletters published by trade or professional associations representing your area of interest. Here are three examples from among hundreds of such newsletters published by associations: the Landscape Architecture News Digest, or Theater Journal, or the American Journal of Computational Linguistics or the newsletter of the American Association of Exporters and Importers. Consult the appropriate association directories listed in the appendix to identify the publications specific to your interests.

WORK EXPERIENCES

A fourth and final method of finding out about the world of work is to sample various work experiences. As a student, you have many opportunities available to you that members of the public at large can rarely consider. Your college years are a time to explore new areas of learning, and work can be one of those areas. Some of your most valuable work experiences may have been other than regular, full-time employment. Experiences such as internships, co-operative education opportunities, volunteer and part-time work, summer jobs and even some extracurricular activities not only give you a chance to test a career interest on a temporary basis, but can serve as marketable experience to help land permanent employment in the same or a related field.

Many employers view experiences such as internships, co-operative education, and summer jobs as "mini-careers," and having one or more of these experiences in your background increases your chances of succeeding at a new position and reduces the risk to an employer in hiring you. If you are still a student, these opportunities are readily available to you and it would be to your advantage to make use of them. You can apply theoretical concepts found in the classroom to real-world experiences in order to enhance your learning and marketability. If you are uncertain about career objectives, a work experience can be an ideal opportunity for you to explore career possibilities. Work experience also provides an important way for you to develop and demonstrate your knowledge, skills and abilities, and personal qualities. Part-time, volunteer, and summer jobs can have the same benefits as some of the more structured learning experiences if goals are initially established, your performance is evaluated, and the experience relates to your career or academic interests.

If you are a recent graduate or soon-to-be graduate, do not overlook the work experiences you had while a student as you reflect upon the factors important to you in your future career.

Internships

Internships cover a broad and varied type of field experience. Internships are intended to provide work opportunities that blend classroom learning with your area of employment interest. The experience may or may not be paid or volunteer, may be awarded academic credit, and may be for varying lengths of time. The experience is related to either educational or career objectives, or both. Internships can range from informal arrangements to highly structured and more formalized programs such as cooperative education. In an internship arrangement, the sponsoring supervisor agrees to take more time than he or she typically would with a new employee to explain the hows and whys of the position, department, and organization. In exchange, you would provide assistance on a project or work activity that complements your education or relates to your career goals. The advantages of internships can be classified according to the developmental opportunities which they provide: cognitive development, career development, and ethical development.

☐ *Cognitive Development*—Internships provide the opportunity to put theory into practice and to apply the knowledge and ideas developed in the classroom to a tangible work situation. This not only adds an important experiential dimension to learning, but often stimulates new interest in classroom learning. Further, internships frequently help the student develop a genuine interdisciplinary perspective.

☐ *Career Development*—Internships also play an important role in developing a greater self understanding and an understanding of the world of work—both crucial to successful career planning. Interning results in:

*Increased awareness and development of skills, abilities, interpersonal competencies, personal qualities, and values.

*The opportunity to test career interests and sample different work environments.

*The opportunity to develop professional contacts.

☐ *Ethical Development*—Internship experiences almost universally bring students face to face with problems, issues, and choices which involve ethical considerations. This opportunity to confront, reflect upon, and resolve important questions of ethical import is another benefit of the internship experience. For example, you might have to decide when and how to tell someone above you in the organization that he or she is wrong or that you feel a certain business practice is contrary to your ethical principles.

SOURCES FOR INTERNSHIPS

There are several internship resource directories that might help you in your search for practical work experience. Ask for them at your library. They include:

☐ Directory of Undergraduate Internships
☐ National Directory of Summer Internships
☐ Directory of Washington Internships
☐ Student Guide to Mass Media Internships
☐ National Directory of Accredited Camps

Other sources include:

☐ Departmentally sponsored internship programs
☐ Formalized internship linkages with local companies
☐ Alumni-sponsored internships
☐ Linkages through informational interviews, family, friends, etc.
☐ Notices in professional publications
☐ Programs through government agencies

Your campus Career Planning and Placement Center will most probably have a file of internship positions which previous students have held. In reviewing these listings or in your efforts to develop your own internship, follow these three steps:

1) DETERMINE INDIVIDUAL GOALS. First, decide what you want to get out of your internship. It is crucial to start with this step instead of jumping immediately to the task of contacting potential employers. Resist the urge to go directly to employers, even though the thinking and research in steps one and two may seem like extra work.

Although the value of any internship is chiefly in the experience it offers, the following questions should still be considered before contacting any employers:

What type of responsibilities do you want to have?

What functions do you want to perform?

What do you most want to learn?

How much time do you want to spend daily or weekly?

Would it be better for you to be a part-time or full-time intern?

How crucial is it for your internship to be paid?

Do you want to earn academic credit for your internship?

2) RESEARCH THE FIELD. Before going to any potential sponsor for your internship, take some time to survey the field of your interest. By looking at career information resources you can obtain a broader scope of possibilities as well as clarify your understanding of what employers are looking for in an intern. In addition, you will increase your knowledge of the field and become familiar with accepted terminology, job titles, etc. Speak to other students who have set up an internship to see how they did it. Talk with employers who have sponsored interns as well as those who might consider sponsoring one to see what they expect from the arrangement. Review the section on People Resources starting on page 46.

3) CONTACT TARGETED EMPLOYERS. The emphasis now switches from what you would like out of an internship to what you can offer as an intern. In addition to your qualifications, consider selling points such as flexibility and initiative. Prepare a proposal for a specific project that you believe an employer needs to have done. Approach the person for whom you would be directly working on the project and try to interest him or her in the possibility of an internship. Contact more than one employer to increase your chances of developing an opportunity.

Why would an employer want to offer an internship? It's important for any prospective intern to consider this question. Some companies clearly use internships as a recruiting tool; they are able to closely review a prospective employee's work over an extended period. The fact that the arrangement is temporary is attractive to many employers since they are under no obligation beyond the agreed upon internship period. In fact, the finite work period may fit in very well with a specific project assignment, or staffing needs created by turnover, temporary absence, or expansion. Employers have used interns to pilot new training programs within their organizations and to introduce on a trial basis other innovations in the organization. They have also used interns for special projects which regular employees do not have the time to complete.

LEARNING CONTRACT GUIDELINES

For an internship to achieve desired goals, it is best to prepare a "learning contract" prior to beginning your experience. Such a contract will clarify your learning expectations for both yourself and your employer and help keep your internship from becoming a traditional employment relationship. Following are key points to keep in mind when developing a learning contract.

LEARNING GOALS. Specifically describe what you hope to achieve and intend to learn through the internship. Write one sentence for each goal and number them in priority of importance to you. These goals might include familiarity with a specific field setting, occupation, or workplace; development of particular skills; increased awareness of concepts such as authority or community; or better understanding of the connections between theory and practice in your chosen field. Is your primary aim gaining, applying, or testing a particular body of knowledge or acquiring or improving a skill? Are you interested in testing a career interest and determining your own suitability for that career? Are you trying to decide what major to choose or what specific courses to take or skills to develop in your remaining years in college? It is acceptable for your goals to be flexible and possibly change at a later time, but it is important to have them to establish a purpose and direction for your learning.

LEARNING STRATEGIES. For each goal you listed, describe what you will do to reach that goal. List several strategies for reaching each goal. For example, will you seek specific reading suggestions from your employer or faculty sponsor? Will you receive any training? If so, what type and for how long? Do you plan to conduct any interviews with other employees in the organization sponsoring your internship? Will you attend any meetings or conferences? Will you visit other employers to obtain a comparison or contrast? Will you receive specific feedback or suggestions on your performance?

EVALUATION METHODS. For each goal, describe how you will know and show others that you have achieved your learning goals. For example, will you keep progress reports or a journal? Will you conduct evaluation sessions with your employer and faculty sponsor? Goals may be re-evaluated mid-way through your internship and adjusted accordingly. Will you make a final presentation or report? Will you share what you learned with other students? Some campuses may even offer a post-evaluation seminar to help you informally review your internship experience.

Check out special requirements if you wish to obtain credit for the internship. Note that if an internship is required by your college program, your one-time internship income is tax-free.

See the following sample worksheet for an example of how to propose learning objectives and methods for accomplishing and evaluating those objectives.

SAMPLE LEARNING OBJECTIVES WORKSHEET

Internship: Legislative Assistant	
Proposed Learning Objectives	**Methods for Accomplishing Learning Objectives/ Evaluation**
Improve writing ability	1) write articles, statements, letters, memos, and other materials 2) review the corrections made on my work by the legislative assistants
Find out to what extent business and economic skills are needed in politics, and determine the other skills that are helpful	1) by reading different publications and seeing what knowledge is needed to understand them 2) by evaluating my written work and what skills and knowledge could have improved my work

Gain a better understanding of the political process	1) by reading publications 2) by asking about different processes and the realities of the success and failure rates 3) by attending hearings and seminars 4) by being involved in the struggle to pass a bill
Learn to cope with a 9–6 job	1) by working to establish good relations with the staff and fellow interns, whether I care for the people or not 2) to discover how to work efficiently throughout such a long day
Help me decide between business and law for my future careers (or to learn both) and find out whether or not I'd be interested in a career in politics	1) by reading publications 2) by speaking to politicians and legislative assistants about their work

Cooperative Education Programs

A special internship arrangement that is more formalized is known as cooperative education. Co-oping integrates classroom study with supervised practical and professional experience in the field. Your academic institution becomes more involved with this type of arrangement in the set-up, monitoring, and evaluation of your experience. Some programs may also require that you return for at least one more academic period of school after completion of a cooperative education internship before you graduate.

A co-op experience helps to give a working knowledge of a particular professional area related to your own academic and career interests before you graduate. It helps to bridge the gap between academic learning and permanent professional employment. The opportunity may help you reaffirm your choice of major or career, it may motivate you to change career or academic direction, or it may convince you that further education (such as graduate school) will help you to achieve your goals.

Summer Jobs and Internships

Like the other activities mentioned in this section, a summer job can be a valuable link in your career development. Besides giving you some income for the summer, it has many of the same benefits as internships and cooperative education experiences.

You should start your summer job search early, even as early as the preceding fall. Many large-scale well-publicized programs such as the U.S. State Department summer opportunities have deadlines in November. Consider spending some time during breaks making contacts for your summer job, especially if you wish to work in the area where you lived before coming to school. See Appendix A for information on finding a summer job in several different career fields.

Part-Time Employment

You can gain valuable experience while in school by working at a part-time job. It is relatively easy to get a part-time position or internship compared to a full-time position, since fewer hours means lower cost. These positions are also somewhat easier for an employer to create. Focus on your area of interest and try to identify a project or routine task needed by an employer. Some students even prefer having several part-time rather than one full-time job because of the increased flexibility.

Do not overlook part-time jobs available on your own campus. Most positions of this type are restricted to fewer than twenty hours per week. Some positions may require campus work-study eligibility but many do not. Check with the student employment office on your campus for eligibility requirements.

Part-time positions are sometimes more abundant than summer positions. Employer needs (except in summer resort areas) usually do not begin and end during the summer when most students are looking for work. If you are considering residing at your school location during the summer, consider taking a part-time position beginning during the academic year which would possibly continue during the summer period and on into other academic years. During the summer you might be able to add a part-time, temporary job to your steady part-time job, or add a part-time, non-paid internship opportunity. Creative packaging may enhance your opportunities!

Volunteer Experience

If you are willing to be a volunteer, there are many work experiences available for which organizations are unable or unwilling to pay. The value to you of such experience is little affected by the lack of pay. Here are just a few examples of the kinds of opportunities available in most communities:

□ *Phone Counselor*—discuss problems and refer callers as needed to other resources.

□ *Researcher*—collect information and interview individuals for a public interest group.

□ *Campaign Worker*—work for a political candidate in a local or state election.

□ *Community Organizer*—help plan lobbying activities and organize community groups to improve their neighborhoods.

□ *Youth Worker*—assist the Salvation Army or a related group in planning youth activities.

In fact, one can offer to volunteer for almost *any* type of work. Volunteer experiences can be easily related to your career interests because you have more choice about the organization you work with and the type of work you do. It is an ideal chance to learn skills that can be transferred to other professional positions at a later date.

Evaluating Student Work Experiences

At the conclusion of your work experience, that experience should be evaluated against the objectives you set prior to beginning an internship or related work assignment. Evaluation should be conducted after the experience to systematically evaluate what was learned. By doing so, you are more likely to avoid mistakes in the next work setting as well as more easily transfer related skills. Your career planning and placement center most likely has evaluation forms that can be of assistance in evaluating your experience.

Any of the work experiences discussed in this unit can also be evaluated on three levels: cognitive, career, and ethical development.

Cognitive Evaluation examines what knowledge you gained and how you learned it, whether that learning was planned or not, and how it relates to your academic experience.

Career Evaluation is consideration of the skills, abilities, interpersonal competencies and personal qualities that you developed or demonstrated and how this experience has helped to clarify your career goals.

Ethical Evaluation examines the life or work values that may have changed as a result of the experience and also reviews how you handled any ethical conflicts that may have arisen in the course of your work experience.

In short, what you learn about yourself and about the world of work is important information that contributes to your career decision making process.

CLARIFYING YOUR CAREER OBJECTIVE

Once you have researched written and computerized resources, had the opportunity to talk with people working in your field of interest, and evaluated your student work experiences, you should have a clearer idea of your career objective. Your career objective should be redefined to reflect the additional information you have learned. For example, if you found that entry-level positions for public relations were very limited, you might broaden your objective to include other liaison positions such as customer and community relations or a more general administrative position. Not only should you have clarified any vague areas of career interest, but you probably will discard (or add) some potential career interests based upon your research.

Your revised career objective will serve as a starting point for the next step, the actual job hunt. You will still be able to change your objective as you learn more about the world of work and your own interests. You also do not have to feel limited to only a single career objective as you start searching for a specific job. Still, it is important to have an objective that is right for you, that is attainable, and that you believe in. Here are some reasons why:

☐ *Sense of Direction*—You will always have a goal that you are working toward and a focus for your job search efforts.

☐ *Elimination of Alternatives*—A clearly defined objective can be as valuable in helping you rule out potential career paths and opportunities, as it is in helping you to select them.

☐ *Preparation for Interviews*—A standard interview question employers will ask is: "What are your career plans?" Having an answer that is clearly and convincingly based on strong knowledge of both yourself and the world of work will obviously be to your advantage.

| **Action Step** | Revise your career objective based on your exploration of the world of work. |

CAREER OBJECTIVE:

CHAPTER *4:*

The Art and Science of Job Hunting

Blue and Gold, 1880

This unit will cover the mechanics of searching for a job. What you learn in this chapter will help get you a position only if you put what you learn into practice. Like any skill, job-hunting needs to be actively practiced to be effectively learned. The advice that follows will work, but only with a sincere, enthusiastic effort on your part. Passively learning this material won't be enough. You need to put what you learn into practice.

THE EMPLOYER'S PERSPECTIVE

Employers are looking for someone who is concerned first and foremost with doing a good job. They want someone who shows an interest in understanding their organization, its needs and goals, and who wants to actively contribute towards those goals. You can best show that you are that type of person by viewing employment opportunities from the employer's perspective.

It is important to identify how any specific job relates to the overall operations of the organization, and how your contribution in a position would help to further the purpose of that organization.

You will be most successful in job hunting if you pay primary attention to the needs of the employer rather than your own needs. This may be difficult if you have pressing financial concerns, for example, but it will be a more effective method for helping you to get the job you want. An employer will hire you not because you need a job, but because you can do a job for the organization. You cannot convince an employer that you can do the job until you fully understand what job needs to be done. You cannot fully understand the job that needs to be done until you view it from the organization's perspective!

Ask yourself and the employer such questions as:

☐ Why is this position open?

☐ If no one was hired to fill this position, what problems would occur?

☐ What are the responsibilities of the position?

☐ What is the relative priority of each responsibility?

☐ How much time should be spent on each?

☐ If someone had the position previously, why did that person leave?

☐ What is that person now doing?

☐ Was that person considered successful? Why?

☐ What changes in the position does the employer envision? Why?

☐ What are the employer's most prominent expectations?

☐ How is performance evaluated?

☐ How does the position relate to the supervisor's job?

☐ How does it relate to other positions in the department?

☐ How does the department relate to the goals of the entire organization?

Asking such questions will demonstrate your level of concern in wanting to do the best job possible for the employer. Your attention will center on the position and the employer's needs and not on yourself. Your frame of mind should be one that projects you into the future as if you were already in the position. Try to imagine what questions or problems you might have if you were to begin the job immediately. Your concern for the employer's need will reflect a mature and professional attitude toward employment.

APPROACHES FOR FINDING JOB OPPORTUNITIES

You can identify job opportunities either through direct approaches or indirect ones. Direct approaches include contacting directly the organizations where you would like to work and using sources such as Career Planning and Placement Centers, employment ads, employment agencies and services, and personnel departments to find information about specific job opportunities that are currently available. Indirect approaches for identifying job opportunities involve primarily talking to individuals in your field of interest to let them know of your interest and availability and to ask their help in your job search. This approach, known as networking, although it may seem less clearly defined, is the one that tends to be the most fruitful for most job hunters, because it enables job hunters to uncover opportunities not widely publicized through the traditional sources of employment information.

Direct Sources of Employment Information

CAREER PLANNING AND PLACEMENT CENTERS

Career Planning and Placement Centers, located on most college and university campuses, can be one of the best sources for identifying specific job openings. Many employers in the area of the campus will list openings with the campus Career Planning and Placement Center, and sometimes do so in lieu of advertising to the general public through newspapers. These employers may be pleased with previous students hired from the campus and wish to establish an on-going relationship, or they may be alumni from the college or university themselves.

Career Planning and Placement Centers offer on-campus recruiting as well as direct job listings for students. National organizations that recruit on campus provide a list of the positions they are seeking to fill and the degrees that would most likely qualify applicants for those openings. The government and other agencies typically provide similar listings. Also available are listings of positions that local employers call or mail into the career planning and placement center. Most opportunities will be conveniently categorized and appropriately dated. So, for example, if you are looking for a part-time position, there will probably be a category just for those positions. In addition, the center may subscribe to one or more job posting systems such as a computerized data bank of employment openings.

Another valuable resource found in Career Planning and Placement Centers is career counselors. They can help you clarify your career goals, locate needed information, identify career opportunities, review your job search strategies, and show you how to do your best in your hunt for the job that is right for you. Most career counselors conduct group workshops on such topics as resume writing, interviewing skills, and job searching strategies as well as doing individual counselling.

EMPLOYMENT ADS

Employment ads advertise specific openings that an organization has to offer. They state the minimum—and sometimes the ideal—qualifications that are necessary for the position. The ads often state the qualifications in the order that they are perceived to be important to the employer. Employment ads are usually found in newspapers or professional journals.

When in newspapers, ads usually reflect the current state of supply and demand in the job market. They are used more heavily by employers when applicants are difficult to find, in highly technical positions, which few people are skilled at, or undesirable positions, which few people want. The quality of the job is often a reflection of where the ad is placed. For example, professional journals will tend to advertise high-level opportunities.

If the ad does not list the employer, it is known as a "blind" ad. Companies may list a blind ad for several reasons. They may do it to avoid communicating their needs and plans to their competition. Such listings may indicate a shift in the company's plans or a gap in the services the company currently has to offer, either of which might give an advantage to a competitor, if they knew of it. An organization may list a blind ad to have evidence for the Equal Employment Opportunity Commission that they advertised a position and were willing to consider any applicant. Or a company may simply use a blind ad to avoid excessive paperwork in replying to all applicants and thus minimize the amount of time spent on filling a specific position. Only the most qualified applicants would be contacted.

EMPLOYMENT AGENCIES AND SERVICES

There are both public and private employment agencies. Public agencies, such as the state employment service, list openings from the government as well as other organizations in the community.

Private agencies are businesses established for the purpose of earning a profit from referral commissions paid to the agency by either the job hunter or the hiring employer. When the fee is paid by the job hunter, the agency usually agrees to assist in preparing the job hunter for finding a job. But only rarely do such agencies provide career counselling for the job hunter and cover many of the topics found in this book. For entry-level positions, such an arrangement is usually disadvantageous, since you would be paying someone else to do what most organizations expect you to be able to do on your own, that is, show the initiative and self-confidence to learn and apply the skills of job hunting on your own.

A greater number of employment agencies earn their money by having employers pay a fee for finding a person to fill a vacant position. The company will list an opening exclusively with an employment agency, and if the agency refers a candidate who is eventually hired, the agency receives a certain percentage (ten to thirty percent) of the individual's annual starting salary. The agency conducts no career counselling, although some preparation for interviews is typically given to the job hunter. Even under such an arrangement, there may be clauses indicating that the individual must pay a fee if for some reason the employer does not pay the fee, or if the individual leaves the organization within the first year of employment. This type of agency tends to favor those job hunters who have specific employment skills that are in high demand, such as secretarial, computer programming, engineering, or other technical skills.

Employment agencies of this type are working for the employer. In this regard, their energies are directed toward filling the positions that they have been given, not toward finding a position for a candidate who has come to them. With this in mind, the job hunter should not place too much reliance on getting a position through an agency.

Certain cautions should be observed if you do intend to work with an employment agency.

1) As already mentioned, be careful of exactly what your contract covers.

2) Also watch out for being persuaded to take a position in which you are really not interested simply because that is what the agency has available.

3) A final caution about employment agencies is that some have been known to advertise positions that do not in fact exist in order to attract you to their service. Such a questionable practice may also be used to obtain resumes of individuals that might then be shown to companies to generate new business for the agency.

On the positive side, agencies can sometimes be the best way to find employment for certain individuals at certain times. The agency might specifically recruit in your area of career interest, in which case it would be appropriate to use. Examples of specialized agencies include: real estate, secretarial, accounting, or computer sciences. An employment agency is more likely to be able to help you once you have two or three years of experience in your career field. Temporary agencies are certainly of value for identifying a wide range of short-term and part-time positions, many of which can turn into permanent, full-time positions in the same organization when you graduate. Yet even in these examples, the cautions still apply.

PERSONNEL DEPARTMENTS

As an organization grows, the level of hiring activity becomes large enough to make it worth while to have a function within the company that is devoted specifically to employment activities. This is the personnel or human resource function. Personnel is a staff function which assists management in publicizing openings and screening and selecting applicants. They typically screen and present the best five or so applicants for each position to the hiring manager for evaluation and ultimate selection. Personnel can influence a hiring decision and quite easily screen out applicants whom they deem to be inappropriate, but the personnel representative rarely makes the ultimate hiring decision.

There are several limitations that a job hunter might have in dealing with personnel departments. One of these is that personnel is often unaware of future employment needs that management might have. For example, a manager might have a customer relations problem that is getting worse each month and costing the company an increasing amount of money in lost business. If the problem becomes serious enough, the potential amount of lost revenue might justify the hiring of an individual to work on the problem. Although the need might have been in the manager's mind for several months—or even years—personnel might not actually have been aware of the need until a specific request for hiring is made and approved. Conceivably, if the manager knows of an individual who is qualified and interested in such a position, that person is likely to have an inside track to the job.

A second limitation of personnel as reported by many job hunters is that they often do not know enough about the specific opening or the working environment of the position to give a candidate a complete picture of what the job entails. Job hunters might not be able to assess or explain their interest in the position or their ability to do the job until the position is discussed with the hiring manager. In such a case, personnel can do a disservice to the company in eliminating a potentially qualified individual from further consideration by management.

People do find jobs through the direct approaches just described, but the majority of individuals get hired through more indirect approaches. Employment ads, agencies and personnel departments are all formal sources of job information. However, they are all public sources, as well. Their job information is readily available to anyone who seeks it. Correspondingly, this means that more people know of such openings and more apply for each opportunity. This makes the competition more intense and the chances of being selected proportionately smaller. For these reasons, using direct sources of employment information alone tends to be quite limited in effectiveness. Of course, you should not overlook any source when you are looking for a job, but avoid devoting too much time to any single approach, especially if that approach is less likely to be effective. As a general rule, spend only a small proportion, say five to ten percent, of your job-hunting efforts on these direct sources of employment information, especially if you are looking for a job in a field where the demand is not particularly high.

Action Step | DIRECT SOURCES FOR JOBS.
Using your career objective as your guide, investigate current job opportunities utilizing sources discussed in the preceding

section, including Career Planning and Placement Center listings, employment ads, employment agencies, etc.

Indirect Job Hunting Methods

Perhaps of greater significance is the fact that most job opportunities, some experts believe as many as eighty to ninety percent, are not listed in such formal sources as those just described. These experts claim that most positions are filled through informal means before they ever become officially announced as being available. In some instances, positions are announced as being formally available after they have already been filled by a candidate of the manager's preference. The position, in such a case, would be announced as being open because doing so is the policy of the organization. In theory, an advertised position allows all qualified people the opportunity to be considered for the position. In practice, however, a manager can easily circumvent such a system by selecting a candidate and then describing qualifications for the position in a way that uniquely matches that candidate's experience and abilities. In other instances, the position is never openly publicized and the manager relies on a network of professional contacts to refer qualified people.

NETWORKING

How does one find out about the job openings that are not formally announced? The best way is through indirect job hunting approaches, the most effective of which is known as networking. Networking allows you to uncover important information through personal contacts that may lead to the position of your choice. Networking gives you an opportunity to get into organizations on an informal basis and learn the needs that exist, or that might or will exist in the future; to evaluate the work atmosphere of the organization; and to learn the ins and outs of employment in your field of interest.

When using people resources to research your field of career interest was discussed in the last unit, it was mentioned that it could serve as the informal start of your job search. People with whom you spoke when you were researching the field can now be contacted for help with specific job leads. But remember, your purpose has changed. In your first discussion you sought information to clarify your career goals. In your subsequent discussion you will seek advice on finding appropriate opportunities.

For example, you can call these same individuals and discuss what you learned and the conclusions that you reached. As part of such a discussion, you can again thank them for the time they took earlier to discuss their work and ask if you could meet with them again to discuss ways that you might best pursue employment within their field.

If indeed you did make a favorable impression on the individual in your first meeting, that person should be willing to give you some further assistance and/or information to help you uncover opportunities. If the discussion went particularly well, the person might even come to be viewed as an organizational friend who can vouch for you to others. Such valuable contacts are much easier to nurture when initially established on the neutral territory of a professional discussion rather than a point-blank request for a job. Once again, in the latter case, it usually appears to employers that you are only interested in yourself and your job—not them and their employment needs. They are also quite likely to be resistant to being put on the spot for a job.

If you did not conduct any such meetings earlier, you can still do some networking now. Approach individuals on an informal basis to specifically seek their help and advice on getting into the field. These individuals can be alumni, referrals from professors, friends, and relatives, names from directories, or even from the yellow pages. Anyone you know or meet is a potential contact. Don't be afraid to ask even those closest to you for help. The more specific you are about the kind of help you need, the more willing and able they are to help. When you call and/or meet with them, discuss your career interests and ask for their advice on who could use someone with your qualifications, how best to uncover appropriate opportunities, and how to pursue such opportunities. You should strive to learn something new with each discussion. Be sincere and forthright in wanting to speak with potential employers for their advice. In many cases, your request will be openly welcomed.

Your efforts should lead to establishing a network of individuals in your desired field of employment whom you have met and with whom you will keep in contact. You can use your network contacts to obtain names of other individuals with whom it might be of value for you to speak. If you ask each person you interview for additional names, you soon will have an extensive list of contacts throughout the field upon which to draw. Such a group of contacts can be of great value in informally watching for opportunities for which you might be eligible, or by giving you the inside story on those job leads you have already identified. These individuals can also be valuable now and later in your future professional career for general advice about work, relationships and problems you will encounter. At times individuals in your network might even be able to directly influence your getting a specific job, either by recommending you for the position, or hiring you themselves in the case where an employment need arises for them.

Here are some suggested questions for your network contacts:

1. Do you think my resume is suitable to apply for this type of position?

2. Do you belong to a professional association? How can I get in touch with the local chapter?

3. Can you suggest sources where I might obtain job listings or announcements for this type of work?

4. What local firms/agencies are most likely to have these kinds of positions?

5. If you were in my position, to which three organizations might you apply first?

6. Do you know of organizations that offer formal training programs for this kind of work?

7. Can you suggest directories or other information in print about employers in this field?

8. Can you refer me to others in the field that might be able to provide me with additional assistance?

9. Is there any other advice or information you would like to add?

10. May I contact you again if other questions arise? Why don't you keep my resume so that you can contact me if you have additional ideas.

Action Step CONTACTS EXERCISE.
Categorize the different contacts you currently have for job hunting. Use space under each heading to fill in names of contacts. Start with people you know and ask for referrals to people they know. (If you are working with a group, don't overlook your fellow group members.) Discuss with them some of the characteristics of your preferred career which you identified earlier in this book. Be sure to get exact spellings of names, titles, business addresses and telephone numbers.

1. Friends and friends of friends:

2. Relatives and friends of relatives:

3. Faculty (within and outside your major):

4. College classmates:

5. High school classmates:

6. People with whom you have worked in community/non-profit organizations or clubs:

7. People with whom you have worked in student organizations or fraternities and sororities:

8. Former employers (part-time, summer, internship supervisors, etc.):

9. Sports partners:

10. Former teachers:

11. College or university advisors:

12. Career Planning and Placement Center staff:

Methods of Approaching Employers

The search for employment is an honorable quest. *Never* feel apologetic or self-conscious about applying for a job. Employers need to hire. Communicate directly and honestly with those who are trying to find qualified applicants. They need you.

APPLYING FOR ADVERTISED OPENINGS

Advertised openings are often located through traditional sources of employment (e.g., Career Planning and Placement Center job listings, classified ads, public and private employment agencies, professional associations).

When applying for advertised openings, consider the following suggestions:

☐ Follow the application instructions carefully. Apply promptly. Be sure all written materials are complete, neat and well written. Whenever possible, type formal applications.

☐ Don't limit your applications only to positions for which you have *all* the stated qualifications. Clearly and specifically state the reasons you are qualified to fill the position. Employers do not always find a "perfect" match and may modify their criteria when they receive a well-prepared application.

□ Note organizations which are advertising many openings at the same time. This may be an indication of expansion, new funding sources, etc. Apply to these employers for possible employment, even if a position of interest to you is not specifically advertised. (Be sure to state your employment interest!)

□ You may apply to the same employer more than once. Even if turned down one time, you may be successful in subsequent attempts.

□ Don't avoid ads which list only a P.O. Box and no employer name. Some employers use this technique to avoid interruptions in their work-places.

□ Whenever possible, reinforce your application with personal contact and/or the recommendation of key contacts.

After you have submitted an application form or resume, it is most appropriate to phone the employer to try to arrange a personal employment interview. If the date you intend to phone is stated in your cover letter, the employer will be alerted that you are seriously interested in employment and will thus be likely to give your resume close attention. If you visit the employer as a primary contact and submit a resume or other application, but are not granted an interview, find out whom you may phone to discuss your qualifications and the most convenient time for you to call.

Whenever you are unable to immediately obtain an interview appointment, be sure that the employer is aware of your continued interest by stating that you would like to contact them again in the near future. Be polite but persistent in your efforts. Don't permit your employment applications to go without periodic follow-up calls. You cannot count on being considered if three months have elapsed since you last made contact.

CAMPUS INTERVIEWS

If you are still a student, take advantage of the opportunity to interview on-campus with employers who have openings consistent with your career goals. See your Career Planning and Placement Center for specific procedures. The number and scope of these interviewing opportunities tend to reflect the supply and demand situation in large organizations and are not representative of the entire job market.

DIRECT APPLICATIONS

Direct application means applying to a potential employer even though a specific position may not be currently advertised. If you are seeking employment locally, your contact may be made by letter, visit, or phone call to the person responsible for hiring in the area of your career interest. A letter and resume are often prepared. You also might visit in person or telephone to inquire about possibilities.

When approaching employers, communicate knowledge of their organization and information about your skills and abilities. Some examples of possible "opening lines":

"I'm interested in possible employment with ABC Corporation. I've reviewed information about your company and am interested in your planning group. Could we schedule an appointment?"

"I have been researching the office supplies industry and am interested in employment opportunities with Better Copies. What procedure should I follow to apply for employment? . . . May I make an appointment? . . . May I send you my resume? . . . When may I phone back?"

"I am impressed with the treatment program your staff uses to counsel depressed youth. I've worked in a similar program and would like to work for such an organization. Could we schedule an appointment?"

"I will complete my degree in Journalism in May. My training has included all aspects of print media. I'm most interested in news coverage. What information do you need to consider me for employment?"

"George Thomas, a broker with your San Jose office, has provided me with very positive feedback about your firm. He said that you are the key person in the hiring process. When could we meet to discuss possible employment?"

"I understand why you might hesitate to fly me to New York for an appointment. When could we schedule a telephone interview?"

"While disappointed that I applied at a time of the year when you are not hiring, I am not discouraged. When might I re-apply?"

CAUTION: These are *only* suggestions and should be revised and tailored to fit specific circumstances and your personal style.

PERSONAL OR PROFESSIONAL REFERRAL

A direct contact is a "key" person who has the power to either hire you or personally recommend to others that you should be hired. You may have developed these contacts through your personal "network" strategy, through personal referral by faculty or professional colleagues, or through informal contacts at professional conferences or meetings. An "interview" might be arranged solely for the purpose of a general discussion of how your background and abilities might be utilized in that organization. Typically, neither you nor the "key" person begins this discussion with a specific job in mind. If there is a possible "match," discussion of specific possibilities might result.

MANAGING YOUR JOB SEARCH

Keeping Organized

A good job hunter has to be well organized! In contacting dozens or even hundreds of potential employers, you need a system of organization and record keeping that allows you to quickly know the status of any given lead at any time.

Index Cards. Some people achieve this organization by using a system of index cards. Each card would have the name, address, and telephone number of an organization you have contacted in your search. It would list the names of those individuals you spoke with and the dates and results of each conversation. Any letters that you sent or received could also easily be noted on the card, as well as the names of referrals you have received. Such a system may sound like a lot of work initially, but the time spent will pay off later in your job search when your memory about the details of any specific call is sketchy or you get a call from someone and can't remember who they are.

```
Data Services Corporation         Referrals:
2555-38th Ave - South
Bloomington, Minneapolis  55440   1. John S. Smith
Gary Cleaver, Manager                ACME Industrial
(504) 556-1212                       Products

                                  2. Zelda Fitzgerald
                                     XYZ Corporation

Date & Nature of Contact          Result:

3/13/84   Wrote Letter
3/28/84   Follow-up phone call    Set up appmt.4/13
4/13/84   Meeting to discuss      Gary will call about
          company needs/my        future openings;also
          qualifications.         gave me referrals.
```

Legal Pad. An alternate approach lists all the contact information on the pages of a notebook or legal pad. For example, before you call any job lead, you might list all such leads down the left-hand side of the page. Then as you make calls, write additional comments on the right-hand side of the page. If someone is not in, you can make a notation in the margin of when to call back. If a prospect does not lead to anything further, you can simply cross out the name, thus maintaining a record of all contacts made. Although this system may be less flexible than index cards, it provides an effective chronological listing of your contacts, which may make finding certain information at a later time easier.

Correspondence File. It is also an easy task to start a correspondence file for job hunting. Make a carbon or photo copy of each letter you write; then as you receive letters you can either attach them to the original letter that you sent, or start a file for incoming correspondence. If correspondence with certain companies becomes extensive, you can easily create a specific file for that company. Such a company file, when combined with additional information about the company such as the annual report and copies of articles about the company, can be very useful in your future contacts.

Time Management

Managing your time effectively is a skill related to your overall organizational ability. To begin with, you must make adequate time for job hunting. Often people make the mistake of being too casual about their job-hunting activities and do not set aside an adequate amount of time to conduct an effective employment search. You will be much more effective in your efforts if you routinely set aside specific hours every day to work on your job hunt. This will not only make the activity seem like less of a chore to you, but it will enable you to predict with confidence exactly when an employer can contact you or you will next contact him. Make sure to include time to reward yourself with recreational and social activities. Allocate your time according to the degree that an activity is likely to generate substantive job leads. For example, do not spend 80 percent of your time looking at newspaper want ads if that activity has only been 10 percent as effective as, say, networking in uncovering possible job opportunities. Here are some basic time management practices which can help you:

1) *Analyze how you spend your time each day.* Find the time available for job-hunting tasks and schedule that time. If possible, try to plan two to three hour blocks of time with minimal interruptions.

2) *Keep a personal calendar which includes all of your commitments.* Mark your calendar with both specific appointments and re-

minders to follow through with return calls, etc. Keep your calendar with you.

3) *Set objectives and priorities.* Make a list each day of tasks to be completed. Mark items on this list which have highest priority and do these first.

4) *Give yourself "do-able" tasks.* Plan in small units (e.g., calling two employers per week). You can only do one thing at a time. If you try to do everything at once, you are setting yourself up to fail.

Telephone Savvy

An often overlooked job-hunting skill is the professional use of a telephone. Although you may have only used telephones for socializing, each individual with whom you speak who works in a business uses the telephone as an important business tool. By using it as a professional would, you indicate that you know what the world of work is all about.

Call Early. You might find that early in the morning and early in the week is the most efficient time to catch people in, although this is likely to vary from person to person as well as from industry to industry. Ask what are the best times for contacting individuals and call back at those times.

If this is the first-time telephone call to a potential employer, before you make your call, take a moment to think with whom you specifically want to speak and for what purpose. Many times if you have been doing extensive telephone calling you can easily lose track of such obvious details—with embarrassing consequences. Be very clear in the first sentence or two about who you are and what you want. Be prepared to answer the predictable questions that a secretary is bound to ask, such as: "What company are you with?" "What is it in regard to?" "Can they call you back?" "Can someone else help you?"

Avoid Messages. One approach is simply to avoid leaving any messages. Many busy people will not return a call from someone they do not know, especially if the purpose of the call is ambiguous. By not leaving a message you have the advantage of not having to explain why you are calling. Simply leave your name and ask when would be a good time to call back. Plan to promptly call back at that time. If you do reach the individual, after you give your brief introduction, ask if it is a good time for the person to talk. By being courteous and sensitive to the other person's position, you are likely to increase your chances of making an initial favorable impression.

Ways to Handle Rejection

Perhaps one of the most valuable skills in job hunting is the ability to handle rejection. It is a skill that is much easier to talk about than to actually practice. The feeling of rejection is an emotional response that is difficult to handle in logical ways. Here are some techniques that job hunters have reported as being helpful to them:

☐ KEEP BUSY. When you receive a rejection, channel the negative feelings into constructive activity that is directed toward your goal. For example, for each rejection letter you receive, file it away and then commit to sending out five more letters of inquiry, or making three more telephone calls that very same day.

☐ TALK TO YOURSELF IN A POSITIVE WAY. We all talk to ourselves mentally or verbally, and what we say can have a significant impact upon our self-esteem and general attitude. Make sure you are not giving yourself negative messages.

☐ DEVELOP MULTIPLE PROSPECTS. By always keeping a variety of prospects in different stages of development, you will have alternatives to pursue. Avoid placing too much faith in any single lead.

☐ TRY TO LEARN FROM "NOs." Try to learn something new from each rejection, something that can help you do better next time. If you do, no interview will ever be a complete loss and you will be constantly improving your technique. You may even ask the person who rejected you for feedback about yourself and how you could improve your chances in competing for future position openings.

Support Groups

Another means of working toward employment is participation in a support group. Such a group meets regularly to discuss progress and problems in each individual's job-hunting efforts. Meetings can be very informal with each person sharing experiences that have been encountered while job hunting since the previous meeting. Problems can be discussed and new approaches suggested. Where possible, role playing can be done to help members of the group who are uneasy about interviewing or using the telephone.

A support group can have many advantages. It can be of great value in handling the negative emotional aspects involved in the process as well as in exchanging suggestions and leads that will benefit other members. Participants' self-esteem typically increases as they help solve each other's job-hunting problems and practice the job-hunting concepts they have learned. The credibility of the techniques is reinforced as members of the group have success with those techniques. The rapport of the group increases as members rely on each other for feedback and support. Participants learn that they have similar concerns and can deal with them in similar ways.

Whether you are still in school or have graduated, you can easily join or start a support group. If you are still in school, chances are that the campus career planning and placement office periodically sets up such groups for interested students. Otherwise, you might form such a group on your own by periodically meeting with friends and acquaintances who are looking for jobs. It only takes three or four people to get started, and such groups usually should not exceed ten or twelve.

When setting up your own group, be sure that everyone agrees with the overall objectives of the group and the guidelines for participation. Support groups tend to be most successful if everyone participating has already developed their career objective, and thus knows the kind of job for which they are looking. Members of the group must make the group a high enough priority to schedule other activities around meetings, and be willing to devote the time to job hunting between group meetings. Members should be willing to share personal job-hunting experiences, whether successful or not, and be supportive of other members of the group. Typically support group members are committed to sharing information and contacts that might be helpful to other members of the group, helping others to diagnose and solve problems related to their job search, and spending a minimum number of hours per week on their own job search. Before the end of each meeting members should outline the action steps each one is committed to taking before the next meeting of the group. This kind of accountability and support can keep you up and going when your job search may have you down.

CHAPTER 5

The Resume and Letter Writing

Blue and Gold, 1881

THE RESUME

There have come to be certain traditional tools that most job hunters use. The resume is one of these. The resume will rarely, if ever, get you a specific job by itself. However, if you do not have a resume or if the one you have is poorly written, you may not be considered for a position. You should strive to have the best resume possible for whenever you might need it in the job-hunting process.

A resume is a written inventory which concisely but forcefully describes your qualifications for a particular job. It encourages clear organization of self-assessment information in a form that is meaningful to employers. It is tailored specifically for the kind of position you are seeking and directly follows from your previously defined career objectives. Its primary purpose is to stimulate the interest of the potential employer enough to want to learn more about you. A resume should present a convincing and realistic picture of your knowledge, skills, abilities, and related personal qualities that would best qualify you for your position of interest. Your resume can be used in a variety of circumstances, including:

☐ To respond to an advertised job vacancy.

☐ To send to an employer that interests you after you have researched an organization.

☐ To accompany formal application forms.

☐ To present to a potential employer at the time of an interview.

☐ To reinforce a personal contact you have already established with an employer.

☐ To accompany requests for on-campus interviews while you are still a student.

☐ To present to a professional association employment committee or conference placement service.

☐ To request that someone write a letter of recommendation for employment for you.

Characteristics of Effective Resumes

An effective resume should:

1. Create a favorable impression.
2. Attract attention to your special abilities and personal qualities.
3. Stimulate interest in you as a person and as a potential employee.
4. Reflect your unique qualifications and assets as much as possible.
5. Be attractive to the eye and professional in appearance.
6. Be literate, demonstrating accurate grammar and spelling.
7. Outline all of your personal assets which support your qualifications for the job you want.
8. Be well organized and concise enough to be read quickly.
9. Encourage the employer to find out more about you.

Developing Your Resume

It can be a difficult task to summarize your life on a piece of paper! You can go about this task several ways. Some individuals initially write down everything they can remember about previous experiences, place the list aside and expand it later on until they feel their list is complete. Other people work best by first discussing their past with a friend or counselor, answering questions that are asked, and then organizing their material in a draft of the resume. Once you have most of your ideas on paper, you can always revise, edit, and improve them. A third and more systematic way of developing your resume is to begin with the type of job you want. This is the method presented in the next action step.

`Action Step` DEVELOPING YOUR RESUME.
Do the following activity on your own and obtain feedback from a friend or career counselor, or, if possible, do it with a group of job hunters.

1) Write out, as clearly as it can be defined at present, your job/career objective.

2) Imagine yourself in the role of an employer hiring for the position you have described in your objective. Brainstorm the qualifications (educational background, skills, abilities, personal qualities) that as an employer, you would be looking for in the person you would like to hire for the position. Here is an example:

OBJECTIVE:	Writer/Editor for a publication produced by a national organization promoting environmental concern.
QUALIFICATIONS:	Proven writing ability Editorial experience Ability to research information Genuine interest in and concern for the environment Creativity Artistic sense

3) Select one of the qualifications you have listed and then quickly review your past life/work/education history and list occasions where you developed or demonstrated that particular qualification.

4) Select one of those experiences, preferably the most positive and important one, and describe it in detail using the following questions as a guide:

What did you do?

How did you do it?

Why did you do it?

What was the result of what you did?

Then add any numbers that would quantify your experience or any adverbs that would help to describe it.

5) Discuss your descriptions with others and ask for a critique.

In developing your resume, keep the following guidelines in mind:

☐ USE AN APPROPRIATE FORMAT. There is no "best" or "right" format for everyone or every situation. The format that you feel best represents you is most likely to serve you the best, as well. Use a format that makes the most important and relevant information about you stand out. It is best to position your information in a descending order from most important to least important. Brevity, neatness and good organization are characteristics of all good resumes. A common resume fault is excessive length. As a student or recent graduate, you should try to confine yourself to a single page. If you go much beyond that length, you may be including irrelevant information or excessive detail. If, however, your experience warrants going beyond a single page, it is better to go to a second page than to sacrifice layout and readability by trying to cram everything onto one page.

☐ FOCUS ON RELEVANT INFORMATION. Try only to include information on your resume that supports your job or career objective. If the relationship is not clear, either explain it or leave the information off your resume. It is not dishonest to skip the fact that you bussed tables during college, if it has nothing to do with your career choice, but on the other hand, if you believe the potential employer would be attracted to the fact that you paid for much or all of your college education by part-time employment, mention it in that context. Relevant information includes any job or educational coursework through which you have developed knowledge and skills appropriate to the job you want. Also included should be any activities, hobbies, part-time or volunteer work experiences which are in some way related to what you want to do. Information that does not reinforce the link between what you can do and the key qualifications for your desired position should be omitted.

☐ FOCUS ON ACCOMPLISHMENTS. Focus on explaining what you have accomplished, not simply what you did or how you spent your time in a position. Achievements show initiative and action—characteristics any employer is looking for in a potential employee. Lay claim to possessing the qualifications needed for the position and then substantiate those claims with specifics from your past. Specifics can include: examples, numbers, percentages, and time periods. It is much more impressive to say: "Designed and implemented a new inventory control system that reduced out of stock items 15 percent in the first month of operation," than simply: "Helped improve inventory control." Where possible, use active, action-oriented verbs like those found on pages 99–100.

Types of Resume Formats

Resume formats can be chronological, functional, or a combination of several types. We will discuss each type and when each is most effective, and provide examples for you to follow.

CHRONOLOGICAL FORMAT

The chronological format, though not necessarily the best format for you, is the most traditional and the one most commonly used. This format gives a chronological listing of all previous experience starting with the most recent position that you held or are currently holding. This format is effective if your most recent work or educational experience is directly related to the type of employment that you are seeking. The general categories listed include: objective, education, experience, and other related experience. Examples of chronological resumes can be found on the next two pages.

SAMPLE CHRONOLOGICAL RESUME

MARY WHITE
1350 BONDO AVENUE
OAKLAND, CA 94611
(415) 555-1234

EMPLOYMENT OBJECTIVE: Management position in branch banking utilizing
organizational, communication, and research skills.

RELATED EXPERIENCE:

PROGRAM DIRECTOR, Vista College/Field Studies Program, Berkeley, CA
Administered innovative experiential learning program. Coordinated
seminars and field placements for 200 undergraduate students. Established and maintained faculty advisory board. Developed fiscal and
course credit mechanisms which assured the continuation of the program.
(9/80 - Present)

COORDINATOR, Martin-for-School-Board Committee, Alameda, CA
Planned, developed and implemented campaign strategy for successful
candidate. Prepared and distributed written information releases to
the media. Designed, developed and executed promotional events.
(5/79 - 11/80)

OPERATIONS SUPERVISOR, Bank of the West, Oakland, CA
Coordinated, trained and evaluated summer personnel in banking operations. Created and implemented cross-training program for summer staff.
(6/78 - 9/78)

MANAGEMENT ASSISTANT, Bechtel Corporation, Contracts Management Division,
San Francisco, CA
Reviewed employment applications. Compiled and prepared written adver-
tising reports. Devised and maintained informational record systems.
Prepared and distributed financial estimates for proposed contracts.
Facilitated communications with staff, clients and subcontractors.
(1/76 - 9/77)

OTHER EXPERIENCE:

TUTOR, Oakland Public Schools, Oakland, CA
Developed and implemented an individualized learning program in reading
for eight- and nine-year-old children. (9/76 - 12/76)

HOST/CASHIER, Benny's Burger Pit, San Leandro, CA
Greeted and seated customers in a busy restaurant. Supervised two
cashiers. Balanced daily cash register receipts and sales. (6/76 - 9/76)

EDUCATION:

UNIVERSITY OF CALIFORNIA, BERKELEY
MA English June, 1979
BA Psychology June, 1977

SPECIAL SKILLS: Communication, organization, training, supervision, evaluation

SAMPLE CHRONOLOGICAL RESUME

KIT JOHNSON

Campus Address: (to 5/30/85)   Alternate Address:

2600 Ridgefield Road   1509 Los Altos Avenue
Berkeley, CA 94709   Long Beach, CA 91804
(415) 555-3213   (213) 555-7901

EDUCATION: University of California, Berkeley, California
                  BA Psychology, May 1985
                  Concentrations: Psychology of Work and Business Administration
                  Honors: Member, Prytanean Society GPA: 3.1/4.0

                  California State University, Hayward, California
                  Sociology Major 1980-1982

EXPERIENCE:

Summers 1984   U.S. NAVAL SUPPLY DEPOT, Oakland, California
        1983   Personnel Clerk: Conducted initial screening interviews
                  for clerical staff. Handled heavy volume of telephone
                  reception. Typed personnel reports and change of status
                  forms.

Summer 1982   DENNY'S RESTAURANT, Hayward, California
                  Hostess: Greeted and seated customers. Supervised
                  two cashiers.

1/80 - 3/82   UNITED ARTISTS' THEATER, Oakland, California
                  Cashier: Sold theater tickets. Prepared opening and
                  closing balance sheets each evening. Answered patrons'
                  telephone inquiries regarding showings.

COMMUNITY
ACTIVITIES:

9/83 - 6/84   ECOLOGY ACTION, Berkeley, California
                  Fund Raising Coordinator: Arranged public forums, scheduled
                  meetings and prepared media releases for a recycling program.
                  Raised $3,000.

9/82 - 6/83   UNIVERSITY YMCA, Berkeley, California
                  Tutor for disadvantaged third graders for the School Resource
                  Volunteer Program.

SPECIAL
SKILLS: Computer languages: FORTRAN, ALGOL; basic statistics;
                  reading knowledge of German.

Willing to travel and/or relocate.

REFERENCES: Available upon request.

FUNCTIONAL RESUME

A functional or skills resume presents information about yourself in a way that emphasizes: 1) those skills that you believe to be most important in the job you seek, and 2) those personal qualities which are among your strongest assets. Such a format is especially desirable if your most recent position does not relate to the position you seek or if you have little or no directly related experience. The primary headings you use with such a resume would include a summary of skills or key skill areas. A more detailed description of each relevant skill would then follow with supporting examples where appropriate. In cases which give extensive detail about categories of skills, your work experience may be shown in an employment history section which lists previous positions, employers, and dates. Your education section, depending on its importance and relevance, might come either before or after the "skills" section. Following are examples of functional resumes.

SAMPLE SKILLS/FUNCTIONAL RESUME

JANICE KNIGHT

3317 Bellevue
Oakland, CA 94610

Home Phone: (415) 555-5831
Work Phone: (415) 555-1725

Objective
: A position using laboratory, data management and research skills in biomedical research.

Skills Summary

LABORATORY
: Performed analytical determinations of chemicals by titrimetry, chromatography and spectrophotometry. Synthesized organic compounds using fractionation, crystallization, and distillation techniques. Analyzed mammalian and plant cell fractions and hormones by gel electrophoresis and bioassays.

DATA MANAGEMENT
: Executed data management and interactive programs to create large computer files in preparation for computer simulations of insect/plant fecundity. Reproduced and interpreted graphs of transformed data.

RESEARCH
: Assisted with curation of zoological specimens. Consulted with investigators on specific research topics. Wrote periodic reports to summarize progress.

Education
: University of California, Berkeley
BA Biology June 1984   Specialization: Cellular Biology

Relevant Coursework:

Cell Physiology	Genetics
Chemistry	Mammalian Physiology/Anatomy
Entomology	Vertebrate Embryology

Special Projects
: Coordinated two-day seminar on genetic research
Volunteer instructor for independent biology course, Berkeley Public Schools
Senior Research: Isolation and Characterization of Plasmid DNA

Experience

Spring 1984
: LAB ASSISTANT, U.S. Dept. of Agriculture, Division of Biological Control, Albany, CA

Summer 1983
: HOSTESS/WAITRESS, Highlands Inn, Carmel, CA

Spring 1983
: LAB ASSISTANT, University of California, Dept. of Biology, Berkeley, CA

Fall 1982
: HOSPITAL AIDE, Children's Hospital, Oakland, CA

Interests
: Cross-country skiing, swimming, cooking, quilting

References
: Available on request

SAMPLE SKILLS/FUNCTIONAL RESUME

```
                          CHRISTINE LEWIS
                  1435 Granite Avenue, Apt. 30
                     Oakland, California 94613
                          (415) 555-5230
```

Skills Summary

RESEARCH   Conducted adult education model program analysis and
                    evaluation for a private research organization. Developed
                    sampling techniques including special variant of standard
                    random sample. Supervised data collection of four survey
                    interviewers. Prepared raw data from computer analysis.
                    Compiled and wrote final reports, including projections
                    and recommendations.

PROGRAM   Devised program outlines for fifteen free university courses,
PLANNING   including writing instructors' manuals, exam formats, and
                    evaluation forms. Assisted with grant proposal development
                    for special experimental education courses.

COMMUNITY   Organized neighborhood association to develop a Cooperative
                    Skills and Services Bank. Planned and conducted meetings,
                    wrote and distributed publicity.

                    Served as fund raising chairperson for local library group.
                    Have raised an average of $5,000/year.

PUBLIC   Have addressed City Council and official city and county
                    committees regarding community projects. Regular substitute
                    hostess for "Issues in Education" radio program. Spokesperson
                    for free university group.

Work History

9/76-Present   S.R.I. International   Educational Researcher
                    Palo Alto, California

8/73-8/75   Heliotrope Free University   Program Planner
                    San Francisco, California

8/72-8/73   Dr. John Brown   Research Assistant
                    U.C. Department of Education

1972-Present   Friends of Oakland Public   Volunteer Organizer
(concurrent)   Library-Oakland Skills and
                    Services Co-op

Education   University of California, Berkeley, California
                    MA Sociology of Education, June 1976

                    California State University, Hayward, California
                    BA Sociology, June 1972

COMBINATION RESUME

Any other combination of the above formats is appropriate if it highlights your abilities in the best way possible for the position sought. For example, a summary of skills could be followed by a description of the one or two most relevant experiences you have had or positions that you have held where these skills were demonstrated. If the positions were several years old, you might even choose to leave off their specific dates or simply include all dates in an "employment history" section.

You should consider using a word processing service and the advice of a friend or placement professional in order to: experiment with different formats and resume content, use different formats and content blocks for different jobs, keep your resume current, and have your resume look professional. In addition, you should run experimental resumes past individuals who have seen many resumes and can offer valuable advice. Attempt to get your resume in front of a lot of people for maximum exposure.

Following are two examples of resumes which use a combined format.

SAMPLE RESUME VARIATION

Scott M. Klein
8 Harrison Avenue
Danville, CA 94526
(415) 555-1234

CAREER
OBJECTIVE: Biologist or Biological Chemist

EDUCATION: UNIVERSITY OF CALIFORNIA, Berkeley, CA
                  BA Biological Science, May 1985

FIELD RELATED
CLASSES:

CHEMISTRY	BIOLOGY
General Chemistry	General Biology
Organic Chemistry	Population Dynamics
Quantitative Analysis	Insect Physiology
Biophysical Chemistry	Independent Research

STATISTICS	PHYSICS
Introductory Statistics	General Physics
Biomedical Statistics	

COMPOSITION	MATHEMATICS
Expository Writing	General Calculus
Practical Writing	

COMPUTER SCIENCE

FORTRAN
PASCAL

WORK
EXPERIENCE: WASTE CONTROL SPECIALISTS, INC., Emeryville, CA
                  Laboratory Technician: Prepared and analyzed soil
                  and water samples for chemical contamination using
                  a gas chromatograph and an atomic spectrograph.
                  (12/82 - Present)

                  STUDENT LEARNING CENTER, University of California,
                  Berkeley, CA
                  Chemistry Tutor: Taught chemistry and problem solving
                  skills to undergraduates; practiced and developed
                  interpersonal skills and problem solving strategies
                  while working with a variety of students of differing
                  abilities and backgrounds. (9/82 - 6/83)

SPECIAL SKILLS: Writing: Popularized science articles, science fiction,
                  lab reports

                  Photography: Black and white portraits, science photo-
                  graphy

                  Computer Science: Translating popular board games into
                                     PASCAL programs

REFERENCES: Available upon request

SAMPLE RESUME VARIATION

```
                        JASON LEE
                  65 Heartvale Street
                  Berkeley, CA  94708
                    (415) 555-6543
```

JOB
OBJECTIVE   Computer Programmer/Analyst

COMPUTER
SKILLS   <u>Languages</u>: COBOL, FORTRAN

                    <u>Coursework</u>: Computer Programming   Accounting
                                Linear Algebra   Economics
                                Differential Equations   Statistics
                                Calculus   Marketing
                                Electronics   Physics

WORK
EXPERIENCE   MARINE INSURANCE CO., San Francisco
                    <u>Coder</u>: Assisted in preparing numerical lists, flow charts,
                    and program outlines for computer applications. (6/84 - 9/84)

                    OLSEN, DEMPSEY & CO., San Francisco
                    <u>Clerk Typist</u>: Coded bills of lading for computer input.
                    Checked output for error. (1/84 - 3/84)

                    YMCA, San Francisco
                    <u>Receptionist</u>: Explained programs to clients. Designed
                    forms. Operated mimeograph machine. (12/82 - 3/83)

                    STUDENT LEARNING CENTER, San Francisco State University
                    <u>Learning Assistant</u>: Evaluated, counseled, and assisted
                    students in overcoming learning skill deficiencies.
                    (4/82 - 9/82)

EDUCATION   University of California, Berkeley
                    BA Sociology, December 1984
                    GPA: 3.3/4.0

COMMUNITY
ACTIVITIES   President of Young Adult Fellowship Council
                    Co-sponsor of Junior Club, YMCA
                    Teacher of junior Sunday School class
                    Volunteer, Herrick Hospital

REFERENCES   References furnished upon request

Standard Resume Content

Regardless of the format selected, resumes should contain certain information:

IDENTIFYING DATA—Name, address (include zip codes), telephone numbers (include area codes).

STATEMENT OF OBJECTIVE—A one or two line description of what you want to do. If used on your resume, this brief description of the type of position desired should be at the top of your resume. If the statement of objective is not placed on the resume, it should be clearly stated in an accompanying cover letter. Different resumes should be written for different objectives so that the content of each resume is tailored to support the objective.

EDUCATION—Name of school, major, degree received, graduation date or projected graduation date. If your degree included courses in areas relevant to your objective, indicate these areas or course titles. Honors and grade point average information is optional, although recommended if considered among your strong points. If you attended more than one school, list the most recent first. It is not always necessary to list all the schools you have attended. Do not list high school unless you have reason to believe it might be helpful (alumni/family/status/etc.). Additional training you have received may either be included here or in a separate category.

EXPERIENCE/WORK HISTORY—Paid or volunteer experience that relates to what you want to do. Emphasize your accomplishments, responsibilities and duties, skills and abilities most appropriate to the position which you are seeking. If the experience does not obviously relate, either drop it or identify some aspect of it that was valuable and relevant, for example, the level of responsibility, research/analytic skills developed, etc. Refer to your skills inventory in Unit Two to be sure your experience as described best matches the skills you say you have. Be sure to include job title and employing organization and dates of employment.

ADDITIONAL INFORMATION—If relevant and appropriate to your objective, the following information should be included on your resume:

☐ Community involvement activities.

☐ Campus activities, such as student organizations or clubs, student government, etc.

☐ Professional affiliations and publications.

☐ Special skills, such as: foreign languages, computer skills, office skills, or other highly marketable assets.

☐ Statement about references—It is acceptable but not necessary to use the phrase "References Available upon Request," or "References Furnished on Request." Ideally your references should be relevant, respected individuals in the career field for which you are applying. Always ask permission before using anyone's name as a reference. Do not use your relatives or your friends as references. Try to use people who know about your work-related abilities, such as former supervisors and faculty members.

You should maintain tight control over how frequently you use your references for two reasons. First, out of courtesy, you do not want your references to be flooded with telephone calls. Second, you might want to contact your references prior to each time they are used to tell them about the position and what the employer is looking for in an applicant. If you do not wish your references to be contacted without your prior approval, be sure to indicate this clearly on any employment applications where references are required.

Style Tips for Resumes

The following is generally accepted good advice for developing an effective resume. Use it in conjunction with the resume examples that are provided in this chapter.

1. Keep it brief and to the point. Long resumes seldom receive much attention and can detract from your effectiveness in the job search.

2. Avoid use of the personal pronoun "I."

3. Use action phrases, especially verbs. They make your resume easier to read and make you seem to be an "action-oriented" individual.

4. Stress accomplishments, responsibilities, and variety of duties performed. Such items give indicators that you can do more of the same.

5. If using the chronological format, list your entries in reverse chronological order beginning with the most recent and working back in time. This is true for both the Education and Experience sections of your resume.

6. If using the skills/functional format, begin with the skill areas most directly related to the position you seek. This maximizes the relevance of your resume to the specific opportunity for which you are applying.

7. New graduates need not be embarrassed about including part-time and summer jobs not directly related to the kind of work desired, but should remember to emphasize the transferable skills and abilities developed or demonstrated.

8. If you have worked for one organization for a long period of time, stress your advancement or progression. Again, this is another indicator that you will likely do the same in the next organization that employs you.

9. It is not necessary to list previous salaries, names of supervisors, or reasons for leaving previous positions. This information can distract from more relevant information.

Resume Layout

1. As a general rule, keep your resume brief enough to fit on one page, or two if your experience is extensive. Edit your resume ruthlessly. If you feel it is too long, ask someone else to suggest material that might be condensed or omitted.

2. Arrange your headings and/or dates in a consistent manner that controls the reader's attention. The key information on your resume, such as previous positions, should be highlighted by bold type, capitalization, or underlining. Employers read many resumes; be sure they can learn the most important facts about you quickly.

3. Bold face or italic type, underlining, and the use of capitalization can highlight important parts of your resume.

4. Make good use of blank space. Well organized spatial arrangement can isolate important points you wish to emphasize; it also adds to the overall impression of neatness and orderliness.

5. Resumes should be on good quality bond paper, either on white or a conservative tone paper such as cream, light gray, or tan. In general, avoid pastels. The quality of the typewriter/word processing printer is also important. Any visible corrections are unacceptable. A good word processing resume service will charge $10–25 for entry and several versions of your resume—money well spent!

6. You will need multiple copies of your resume. Check with copy service rates and reproduction methods. Many printers offer resume specials which include matching envelopes and extra blank stationery for cover letters. Printing is usually only cost-effective if you make over 50–75 copies. Do not order too many copies at any one time, since you will be reluctant to make changes when they become necessary. Word processing with letter quality printing is a much better alternative, especially since it allows for easier changes and improvements. Save the original copy of your resume so that you can easily reproduce more at a later time.

7. Before reproducing your resume, be sure to have several people who are experienced proofread the final draft for typos, misspellings and the accuracy of numbers, especially address and telephone numbers. Careless mistakes on your resume are inexcusable!

ACTION VERB LIST FOR RESUMES

The following verbs can be used to describe your previous experience in an active fashion. Use the present tense of the verb for current employment and the past tense for previous employment. This list is not exhaustive, so feel free to use other action verbs which may better describe your experience.

accomplish
achieve
add
adjust
administer
adopt
advise
advocate
aid
allocate
analyze
applied
appraise
approve
arbitrate
arrange
assemble
assess
assign
assist
attain
audit

budget

calibrate
care
change
check
clarify
classify
coach
code
collate
collect
communicate
compete
compile

complete
compose
compute
conduct
confront
consolidate
construct
control
coordinate
correspond
counsel
create
critique

decide
delegate
demonstrate
describe
design
determine
develop
diagnose
differentiate
dispatch
dispense
display
dissect
distribute
document
draft
draw

earn
edit
educate
effect
encourage
enlist

establish
estimate
evaluate
examine
exhibit
expedite
explain
express

facilitate
forecast
fulfill

generate
guide

hire

identify
implement
induce
influence
inform
initiate
illustrate
imagine
inspect
inspire
install
instruct
integrate
interpret
interview
invent
investigate
involve

judge

launch
lead
lecture
lobby
locate

maintain
manage
map
measure
mediate
mentor
model
monitor
motivate

navigate
negotiate

observe
organize
originate

participate
perform
persuade
plan
predict
prepare
present
print
prioritize
process

produce
program
project
promote
proofread
propose
provide
publish

question

raise
recommend
reconcile
record
recruit
reduce
refer
regulate
rehabilitate
reorganize
repair
replace
replenish
report
represent
research
resolve
respond
revamp
review
revise

rewrite

schedule
secure
select
sell
serve
simplify
sketch
solve
speak
streamline
strengthen
succeed
summarize
supervise
synthesize
systematize

teach
theorize
train
transfer
translate
treat
troubleshoot

update
upgrade

verify

write

LETTER WRITING

There are numerous occasions for you to use writing skills in your job hunting activities. In many cases, writing may be the only vehicle through which a potential employer knows you. It is an important skill to be able to express yourself well whenever your job hunt requires it.

Although most people looking for employment will claim to have excellent writing abilities, far fewer of them actually demonstrate the skill in their job hunt.

Every letter provides an opportunity to make a good impression on the recipient. As an applicant seeking employment, you will find yourself writing different types of letters for different occasions. Each should follow proper business form and format. However, each letter should be adapted to the occasion and the specific person to whom you are writing. The letter should be addressed to a specific person in the organization you are contacting and individually signed by you. Following are explanations of the most commonly used types of letters, along with some examples.

Inquiry Letters

An inquiry letter is a simple request for information. You may request an annual report or descriptive brochure of the company. You may request the names of persons to whom you could direct further inquiries of a more specific nature. For example, you may write to the Advertising Club of San Francisco and request the names of two or three members who might be willing to give you information regarding employment prospects in "point-of-sales" advertising.

Cover Letters

A cover letter is one that accompanies your resume or application for a specific position. It should arouse interest in you as a candidate and emphasize the aspects of your abilities and past experience which are most impressive and relevant to the job. Separate cover letters should be prepared for each potential employer and your resume tailored to the specific type of opportunity that you are seeking. Below is a description of how to structure a cover letter.

OPENING—Start your letter in a way that will get the reader's attention and interest. State your purpose for writing.

BODY—Appeal to the person's self-interest. State why the employer should be interested in you. Ask yourself: "What can I do for this organization?" Explain the relevant details of your qualifications. Back up your claims with specific examples.

CLOSING—Indicate your hope for a personal meeting and tell the person how you intend to follow up on the letter.

SAMPLE COVER LETTER

25 Florence Drive
El Cerrito, CA 94530
(415) 555-2999
November 5, 1984

Ms. Sheila Foxworth
Senior Employment Representative
RIA Laboratories, Inc.
25 R Street
Oakland, CA 94660

Dear Ms. Foxworth:

Dr. Klein, in the U.C. Berkeley Microbiology Department, has informed me of your laboratory expansion plans. Since you are extensively involved in research using monoclonal antibodies, I am very interested in an entry-level laboratory position with your organization. I will receive my Bachelor's Degree in Microbiology from U.C. Berkeley in May 1985, and will be available to begin work on August 1.

I have performed two independent research studies at the Lawrence Berkeley Laboratory, both of which involved the use of a wide variety of laboratory equipment and procedures. In addition, I have worked closely and effectively with other research personnel. My analytical skills and writing ability have been developed through coursework and my practical experiences.

I have enclosed my resume and course list, which outline my qualifications in further detail. I would welcome an opportunity to discuss my qualifications and the possibility of future employment with you. I will phone you within eight to ten days to see if an appointment can be arranged.

Very truly yours,

Angela Rios

Angela Rios

Enclosures

A SPECIFIC POSITION OPENING

POSITION OPENING

Job Title: RESEARCH ANALYST

Job Description: Requirements for this position include a BS or BA degree in business or the social sciences with emphasis in marketing research, consumer behavior and quantitative methods; professional experience in survey research and/or programming and use of interactive timesharing applications; initiative, resourcefulness, thoroughness and responsibility in independent work; the ability to deal effectively with people; good written and oral communication skills; the ability to analyze and evaluate quantitative and subjective data.

COVER LETTER IN RESPONSE TO POSITION OPENING

65 Heartvale Avenue
Berkeley, CA 94708
(415) 987-6543
March 30, 1985

Ms. Carol MacDonald
Safeway Stores
201-4th Street
Oakland, CA 94660

Dear Ms. MacDonald:

Through the Career Planning and Placement Center at U.C.
Berkeley, I learned of your opening for a Research Analyst in your
Oakland office. Please consider the enclosed resume as an appli-
cation for this position.

My educational background in marketing and computer science,
along with my quantitative skills, make me especially qualified for
your position. I am also familiar with and have programmed in COBOL
and FORTRAN computer languages.

I work well independently, prioritize in an efficient manner,
and communicate easily with all types of people. My analytical
skills have been demonstrated through experience in coding information for computer input and checking output for accuracy.

At your earliest convenience, I would appreciate discussing my
qualifications with you. I will call you within the week to
schedule an interview.

Sincerely,

Jason Lee

Jason Lee

Enclosure

Letter in Lieu of Resume

Some experts believe that a well written letter which includes the high points of your qualifications for a specific opening can effectively take the place of a resume altogether. Such a letter should be used if you feel you will better stand out from the bulk of resumes that are being submitted for the position. This "narrative resume" would touch on the key categories found in most resumes, yet be specifically tailored for each job lead. This type of letter should be sent directly to the person responsible for hiring for the position you seek.

LETTER IN LIEU OF RESUME

97403 Westchester Avenue
Chicago, Illinois 60640
(312) 555-4100

October 12, 1984

Mr. Jack Clemmons, Sr.
Manager, Staywell Program
Data Services Corporation
2655-138th Avenue West
Bloomington, MN 55440

Dear Mr. Clemmons:

I am confident that my technical expertise and dedication to
physical fitness can be combined to provide an invaluable contribution to the staff of the Staywell Employee Health Program.

As an assistant cost analyst for one of the leading developers
of radar systems for aircraft, I was responsible for researching
new business proposals, coordinating technical data and specifica-
tions, and proposal preparation. I worked with contracts of all
sizes and interacted extensively with upper management of the
organization.

I have first-hand experience with the benefits and difficulties
of pursuing physical fitness. I was an alpine ski instructor for
over five years. As part of my interest, I have written about
the philosophy and techniques of teaching skiing.

In addition, my administrative experience as a management intern
while attending Stenvens Institute of Technology has given me
valuable insight into the world of business and the practicalities
of office operations.

I would like to explain further the relevance of this and other
experience I have had in a personal meeting at your convenience.
I will contact you shortly to see if such a meeting can be
arranged.

Sincerely,

Mark Schmidt

Mark Schmidt

Thank-You Letters

Thank-you letters after informational or job interviews are important. They are a way to show that you are still interested in a specific position, add information that you might have forgotten in your earlier discussion, and generally indicate that you are well-mannered and professional in your approach to the job search.

THANK-YOU FOR A SECOND INTERVIEW

100 Acme Avenue
Middletown, CA 94123
(415) 555-1256
April 2, 1985

Mr. Donald J. Brown
Administrative Coordinator
Business and Technical Personnel
Consolidated Engineering, Inc.
900 East Fourth Avenue
Sunnyvale, CA 94087

Dear Mr. Brown:

Thank you for the opportunity to spend last Thursday at your manufacturing facility in Sunnyvale. The discussion we had was particularly informative. I found the tour of your plant and the informal conversations with your engineering staff to be quite beneficial.

I was very impressed with the effective manner in which Consolidated Engineering, Inc., has adapted the management-by-objective system to their technical operations. This philosophy suits my interests and training.

The entire experience has confirmed my interest in Consolidated Engineering, and I look forward to hearing from you soon.

Sincerely,

George S. Moore

George S. Moore

Follow-up Letters

A follow-up letter is one that you might send after a thank-you letter if there has been a delay in hearing from an employer. It should be polite and positive, restating your interest in the position and asking for a report on the status of the selection process. A similar type of letter is one that seeks to clarify a specific aspect of your interaction with the employer. In such circumstances, however, a telephone call might be even better. It is evidence of the importance you place on the information you are seeking and allows for a more immediate and personalized response to your request.

SAMPLE FOLLOW-UP LETTER

```
                                  158 Saint George Drive
                                  Berkeley, CA 94705
                                  (415) 555-1278
                                  April 20, 1985


Ms. Zelda Fitzgerald
Director of Corporate Recruitment
XYZ Corporation
3123 Market Street
San Francisco, CA 94101

Dear Ms. Fitzgerald:

     I contacted your office three months ago seeking employment
as a Marketing Representative in your Sportswear Division.  Because
a major reorganization was in progress at that time, you suggested
I recontact you in three months, when the personnel staffing needs
of that division would be finalized.

     It is my understanding from reading the article in Tuesday's
Wall Street Journal that this reorganization has been successfully
completed.  Consequently, I would like to take this opportunity to
restate my interest in employment as a Marketing Representative in
the newly reorganized Sportswear Division.

     Because some time has passed since I initially submitted my
application materials, I have attached an updated copy of my resume
for your review.  Since our last conversation, I have successfully
completed the marketing course you suggested at U.C. Extension.
That course, coupled with my prior work experience, has provided
me with the skills and abilities necessary to make an effective
contribution to the marketing functions of your Sportswear Division.

     Please consider me for employment should any openings occur.
I will call you in a week to inquire about your hiring plans.

                                  Cordially,

                                  Martin Yoshida

                                  Martin Yoshida


Enclosures
```

Acknowledgement Letters

An acknowledgement letter is used to formally accept or reject an offer. If accepting an offer, you should indicate a date on which you are available to begin work.

After accepting an offer you should also send letters of regret to any employers who are still considering you for employment. Writing this type of letter is good business practice. It is a courtesy to these employers as well as an opportunity to thank them for their time and interest in considering you for employment.

SAMPLE ACKNOWLEDGEMENT LETTER

```
                                          1400 Olsen Highway
                                          Whiteside, CA 94962
                                          May 20, 198-


        Mr. John Smith, Manager
        ACME Industrial Engineers
        734 Metro Boulevard
        Billings, MT 67321

        Dear Mr. Smith:

        This is to inform you that I will be unable to accept your offer
        for employment indicated in your letter of May 12.  Although the
        position and your firm held great interest for me, after deliber-
        ation I have decided to accept an offer from another firm.  Best
        of luck in finding a suitable candidate for your employment needs.

                                   Sincerely,

                                   David Jackson
                                   David Jackson
```

Reference Letters

Reference letters are less commonly used today in job hunting with the exception of certain fields such as education, nursing, and librarianship. If you have a letter from a previous employer, it would probably be an item to bring with you to an interview and use if the need arises. The best reference letters are ones that are specific about the things you accomplished in a previous job. Good reference letters avoid broad, general statements that are unsubstantiated and could easily apply to most applicants. You can help the person you ask to write a reference letter by providing a summary description of items that might be commented on. For example, for a professor you might list the projects or papers done and some of the comments noted by the professor about each.

APPLICATIONS

Many employers will require you to fill out an employment application at some point in the hiring process. A number of the items will be a duplication of information provided on your resume, but you will often be required to fill out the application just the same. If possible, take the application with you and type in the necessary information at home. Even if you restate all the information on your resume, you should attach a copy of your resume to any application that you complete. This will insure that your information will be presented in the form, sequence, wording and appearance that are best for you.

CHAPTER 6:
The Interview

Blue and Gold, 1891

T he personal interview is a structured exchange of information between two or more people for the purpose of further communicating qualifications for a position. It is also an opportunity for you to assess your desire to work for a specific employer. As employers interview job applicants, they are looking for evidence that a candidate can perform the tasks of the position and fit in well with the organization and the department. In addition to specific qualifications, the interviewer is often influenced by the personal qualities of the applicant as detected in the interview. The interviewer, in general, will be looking for:

☐ Self-concept—The candidate's ability to display self-confidence, goal setting, realistic assessment of strengths and limitations.

☐ Maturity and judgement.

☐ Communications skills, including the ability to interact effectively with others.

☐ Leadership potential—such as demonstrated in extracurricular activities or on previous jobs.

☐ Personality—enthusiasm, poise, cheerfulness, flexibility, sense of humor.

☐ Patterns of accomplishment.

☐ Problem solving and analytical abilities.

☐ Interest in and knowledge of the career field.

☐ Work ethic—acceptance of responsibility and ability to keep commitments.

☐ Appearance—dress, grooming.

☐ Level of skill and knowledge appropriate to particular job functions.

These items will be assessed in a structured interview that usually follows a fairly standard pattern. The interview begins with an introduction and exchange of small talk to put both individuals at ease. These first few minutes can be important to your success, since people often form lasting impressions about others very quickly. The interview will proceed with a discussion of your background, including your work experience, education, extra-curricular activities, etc.; a discussion of the skills and related abilities you have to offer; additional commentary on the job, work environment, organization, etc.; opportunity for questions; and a closing.

Preparing for an Interview

You can best prepare for an interview by doing some research on the organization and the specific job opening and then reviewing your background, especially as it relates to the requirements of this particular position. Be able to clearly explain your career goals and how you arrived at them. Analyze your strengths and weaknesses and be able to give examples of each. Know what you want to communicate and how you want to communicate it. Role play a practice interview with a friend. When you research the employer, learn as much as you can about the organization's history and background: what it does, the services and products it offers, where its branches are, what its future prospects are, etc. Read any of the organization's brochures and past annual reports. Check the *Reader's Guide to Periodical Literature* or the *Business Periodical Index* for recent articles in such publications as the *Wall Street Journal, Business Week, Fortune,* and *Forbes* or other publications specific to the industry. Consult a reference librarian for ways to find additional information. If you cannot find much information about a specific organization, at least learn as much as you can about the industry in general. A useful reference for this purpose is the *U.S. Industrial Outlook* published by the U.S. Government Printing Office. Do not expect employers to educate you about their organizations!

Conducting the Interview

At the risk of stating the obvious, here are some generally accepted ground rules for the interview. Unfortunately, they include many mistakes commonly made by students.

Give yourself enough time to arrive at least fifteen minutes early for the interview.

Dress appropriately.

Use a firm handshake.

Be enthusiastic and interested about the occasion.

Maintain good eye contact with the interviewer.

Avoid smoking or chewing gum.

Introduce examples of your work experience into the conversation as appropriate.

Focus on the positive aspects of your previous jobs.

Do not belittle yourself or any of your previous employers.

Listen to a question before answering it. Avoid just answering with "yes" or "no." After you answer a question, you may want to pursue a related point by asking a question of your own so that the interview does not become one-sided.

Below are some common interview questions with some suggestions for developing responses:

☐ *What are your career plans?* This question is asked to see how your future plans mesh with those of the company. The interviewer wants to know if the job under discussion meets your short-range goals or fits well with your future career goals.

☐ *Why are you interested in this organization?* The employer is asking this question to determine: 1) How much you know about the industry, and 2) How much research you have done about the specific firm. Often the response to this question is complimentary to the company's reputation in their industry. More importantly, you should be able to articulate how your career plans are compatible with the company or organization with which you are interviewing.

☐ *How did you choose your major and this university?* Employers are trying to determine your decision-making process. Tell about the thoughts that went into your decision and the factors you considered in making it. Employers are interested in learning how you make decisions and what you consider important.

☐ *Tell me about yourself.* The employer is asking you for a profile of yourself in order to compare it with profiles of successful company employees. Be factual. Discuss the qualifications that make you feel that you will be successful in your career. Indicate how you have developed these qualifications and talk about the people, things, and ideas that have motivated you to pursue your chosen career path.

☐ *What other employers do you plan to interview with?* The employer asks this question to determine how interested you are in their particular industry or related industries. Tell which comparable organizations and similar types of jobs you have investigated.

☐ *What are your greatest strengths? What are your chief weaknesses?* The employer asks these questions to determine what your self-image is. This is an opportunity to point out all of the strengths acquired through your past jobs and campus and community activities, and relate them to the employer's needs. Do not dwell on negative items. Briefly mention a weakness that you are taking steps to overcome or have already overcome. Employers look for the ability to overcome difficulties. Concentrate on strengths and weaknesses related to the work environment.

Handling Discriminatory Questions

In the past when you encountered what you felt to be a discriminatory question in a job interview, you had to decide whether you wanted to answer the question and feel uncomfortable, or refuse to answer the question and possibly lose your chances for the job.

It may help to know a little bit about the kinds of questions that can be considered discriminatory, and the reasons why they have often been asked. Having this information will help you think about how you might respond.

CAUTION: We make no pretense of being lawyers. Detailed information on applicable laws may be sought through the Fair Employment Practices Commission (FEPC), the Equal Employment Opportunity Commission (EEOC), or an attorney. Your Career Planning and Placement adviser may have additional information.

Questions such as the following can, in some instances, be considered discriminatory when asked of a female applicant and not a male applicant seeking a similar job. Questions about: marital status, marital plans, plans to have children, child care arrangements. Understanding why these questions have been asked in the past can provide clues about how to deal with them now. Some examples:

☐ *Traditional sex-role stereotypes.* Is the question relevant to the position at hand? Ask why the individual needs to know, and if the need is legitimate, attempt to accommodate it.

☐ *Legitimate need for information.* For example, questions regarding marital plans and/or status have often been aimed at determining the degree of long-term career commitment. The underlying questions in these examples are legitimate, but the overt questions are not.

Do not try to make an issue of the questions (even though they may be irrelevant and discriminatory). Make your answer concise; such as, "I have given my career plans much thought and preparation. I am confident that my personal plans will not interfere with my job (career plans)." This type of response answers the interviewer's question; however, it makes it clear that your personal life will not interfere with your work performance.

If a question seems discriminatory, try to determine how it relates to the job and then answer on that basis. For example, "Will you have to drop off your children at day care in the mornings?" might seem like a random, unnecessary question unless the employer is especially concerned with having you arrive at work on time. Your reply can be: "I'll have no difficulty arriving at work by 8 a.m."

| Action Step | FREQUENTLY ASKED INTERVIEW QUESTIONS.* Think about the following questions, which are among those likely to be asked in your interview. Prepare your answers in advance. Consider writing out your responses to help you fully develop them prior to an interview.

☐ In what school activities have you participated? Why? Which did you enjoy the most?

☐ Do you feel you have done the best scholastic work of which you are capable?

☐ How did you happen to go to college?

☐ What qualifications do you have that you feel will lead to success in your career?

☐ What have you learned from some of the jobs you have had?

☐ What kind of boss do you prefer?

☐ How did previous employers treat you?

☐ What kind of work interests you?

☐ Are you willing to travel?

☐ Are you willing to work overtime?

☐ What have you done that shows initiative and willingness to work?

☐ What kinds of books have you read?

☐ Have you plans for graduate study?

*Adapted from a survey of companies by Frank S. Endicott, former Director of Placement at Northwestern University.

☐ What do you like about work?

☐ With what kinds of people do you work best?

Action Step INTERVIEWING ROLE PLAY.
          Practice interviewing by role-playing with a friend.
Have your friend play the interviewer. Provide him or her with information
about the organization and the position for which you will be interviewing.
Ask your friend to use some of the frequently asked questions above. If
possible, video-tape the practice session and critique it together following
the interview. Use the following check list if you are able to video-tape
the practice interview, or discuss these questions with your friend to learn
his or her impression of your interview style:

Are your entrance and handshake positive?

Do you appear to be poised and self-assured?

Is your grooming up to your standards?

Do you think you project a positive image of yourself?

Could you have dealt more effectively with questions that were asked?

What does your body language say?

Is it passive?

Does it project energy?

Does it project vitality?

Are you leaning into the interview?

Are you establishing good eye contact?

Are your hand gestures expressive—rather than stilted or exaggerated?

Do you appear poised and relaxed?

Is your voice well-modulated?

Does your voice reveal your true vitality?

Are you communicating in complete sentences?

Are you contributing important information about yourself?

Are you a good listener?

Does your exit leave a positive impression?

Questions You May Ask

An interview should be an exchange of information. You should have questions formulated to ask an interviewer so that you can make an intelligent decision about accepting the position if offered. If you do not get a chance to ask questions during the main portion of the interview, you will likely have a chance at the end of your discussion. The specific questions you should ask will vary from organization to organization, but be sure to ask questions that focus on the job, its responsibilities and opportunities. Questions about benefits, vacation, etc. are better asked during subsequent interviews or after a job has been offered.

| Action Step | QUESTIONS TO ASK IN INTERVIEWS.
Review the following questions, which you might consider asking during your interview. Choose the ones you feel are important to ask if they are not answered during the course of the interview.

What are the day-to-day responsibilities of this position?

Do you have a formal training program? If yes, how long is it and could you describe the type of training provided?

How will my performance be evaluated, and how often?

What would be a typical career path for an employee like myself entering your organization?

To whom would I report? Under whose supervision would I be assigned?

Would I be responsible for supervising other staff? If so, how many and what positions?

How is the present economic situation affecting your organization?

What are your plans for expansion in terms of product lines, services, new branches, etc.?

What new products will be introduced in the near future as a result of research and development?

How would you differentiate your company from your major competitors?

What do you consider to be the major problems facing the industry today?

Closing the Interview

Do not linger when the interview is over. Ask if there is anything else the interviewer wants to know. Reiterate your interest in the position. Ask what the next step is and if you should contact the person. Ask when you may expect a decision. Be sure you have the interviewer's name and business address. (Ask for a business card.) Thank the interviewer for his or her time.

Using References

When an employer becomes interested in you as a candidate, they will likely want one or more references they can contact. References are used to confirm the things you have said about yourself and your background. The ones that have the most impact are those from previous supervisors, especially the supervisor from your last job. If you have not worked recently, a professor who knows you well will do equally well, especially if that person is in your field of interest. Avoid using individuals who have not seen you in a work setting. Do not use relatives, personal friends, etc.

Line your references up in advance. Ask anyone you are considering if they would be willing to serve as a reference for you. Most people will accept, although some will decline if they feel they do not know you well enough. Discuss with them your career plans and the type of position you are currently seeking. As you are asked for your references by employers, let your references know who is likely to give them a call. Help your references and yourself by briefing them on the specifics of the position, the organization and the aspects of your background in which the employer is most likely to be interested.

As a courtesy to your references, don't give out their names to more people than necessary. Some organizations routinely check all references of applicants PRIOR to interviews. Having your references receive too many calls is abusive of the favor they are doing for you. Do not put the names on your resume, but instead wait until you are asked for them or have to provide them on an application.

Handling a Panel Interview

Panel interviews are those conducted by a group of three to fifteen people. They are common with positions in government and educational institutions. Not all members of the panel are there to evaluate your qualifications. Some members may just be interested in your views on the school, agency or community.

Be a good listener, answer questions briefly and let the panel determine the direction of the interview. Panel interviews are often conducted under tight time constraints (perhaps every fifteen minutes), so take special care to give concise answers. When asked questions by several members at once, pause, think, and respond to one question at a time. You may need to ask that a question be restated. Begin and end your response by directly addressing the person who asked the question. If it is a long response, try to establish eye contact with as many of the other members of the panel as possible.

The Second Interview

If your first interview is successful, you will be asked for a second interview for further evaluation. The following suggestions can assist you in planning for and handling this interview with confidence.

PREPARING FOR YOUR VISIT

If you are traveling out of town be sure to make arrangements in advance. The company will usually pay your expenses if it is a second interview. Be sure you know the logistics involved before you leave. Will the company representative make reservations for you (airline? hotel? car?) or are you expected to do this? If it is up to you, consult a travel agent. You need to be as rested as possible on the day of your interview and so should minimize the stress caused by travel arrangements. Second interviews usually last the better part of a day, so don't plan anything else for that day.

Whatever your expenses are, be sure to keep receipts for your own taxes or to submit to the company's accounting office. Some companies reimburse you at the time of your visit. They "walk" your papers through accounting, and give you a check at the end of the day. Do not expect cash. Other companies mail you the reimbursement. If you are visiting two companies on the same trip and they have both offered to finance the trip, you should notify each company so that they may share the expense of your visit.

Complete any necessary employer forms and send them in advance of your arrival. It is a good idea to bring copies of these forms with you as well as extra copies of your resume. Plan your wardrobe. Bring a small notebook with you. Re-read company literature and jot down further questions that you may have. Call the person who invited you back if you have additional items that need to be clarified for the second interview.

THE DAY OF YOUR VISIT

At the onset, be sure you understand the position for which you are interviewing. A typical progression might start at the organization's personnel office and a chat with the recruiter with whom you initially met. You will probably then meet with your potential supervisor, that person's manager, and other co-workers. At the end of the day there may be a final conference with a personnel representative.

Some firms provide you with a typed agenda of the day's interviews, giving the name, title, and areas of responsibility of each person with whom you will be talking. Try to understand how each person on your schedule relates to the others. If you are not provided with this information, ask for it and take notes. It's very important that you ask questions throughout the day; this will demonstrate your interest and knowledge of the organization.

Be prepared for different types of interviews including the "pragmatic" interview. In it an employer may outline a problem which the company is currently facing and ask you for suggestions on how to solve it. Remember that most employers really do not expect a solution, but are more interested in the way you approach the problem and analyze possible alternatives. Always ask for more information about the situation, before formulating your response.

Although less commonly used today, another type of interview is the "stress" interview. The stress interview is intentionally difficult. Stay calm and think carefully about your responses. Do not be afraid to take time to think through your answers. The object of the stress interview is to evaluate your behavior and maturity in difficult situations. Such an interview may come at the end of the day when you are tired and feel most defenseless.

Some firms use psychological testing. These are usually written tests, and are designed to evaluate your suitability for a particular type of assignment—sales, for example. These too have become less common in recent years.

Employers will be looking to evaluate you on qualitative aspects such as your social skills and degree of motivation. They may arrange to see you in different situations such as in a meeting or at lunch or dinner. Questions might be asked extensively about your outside interests. Be polite and responsive.

FOLLOW-UP

If you do receive a verbal offer, you should certainly express your interest, but it is probably best to ask for some time to consider the offer, especially if you are hoping for offers from other organizations as well. It is always a good idea to request a written confirmation of the offer. Such a letter will probably cover fringe benefits, moving arrangements, etc. Discuss with the company an acceptable time frame in which to make your decision.

When you return home, take time to write a letter of appreciation. This will also demonstrate your continued interest in the opportunity. If you do not hear from the employer within two to three weeks, you should call to inquire about the status of your candidacy.

HOW TO BE AN "IDEAL" CANDIDATE EVEN IF YOU'RE NOT

Employers hope to hire applicants that seem to be nearly a perfect match for their open positions. Yet the screening process focuses first on looking for reasons to eliminate applicants in order to arrive at a manageable number to interview for each position, say five to seven individuals. To the extent that those candidates can quickly be identified from among all who apply, the job can be filled sooner and the work can continue.

This all means that the initial screening process is apt to be very general in order to exclude broad categories of candidates. This is why seemingly small factors, such as a misspelled word on your resume, can have a significant effect on your chances of success. The same is true for other details throughout your interactions with a potential employer. Here are some guidelines for how to be the best candidate you are capable of being.

BE DYNAMIC

The best job hunters convey a strong self-confidence. They are persuasive and good at selling themselves to others. Even if this is not your style, focus on being enthusiastic and you will find it will be contagious. Often job hunters present themselves as only being average candidates, whereas with minimal effort they could easily be quite impressive. For example, if your resume does not stand out from most of the other resumes that you have seen, focus on how it could be more impressive. You could brainstorm about possible improvements on your own, with a friend, or with a counselor in your Career Planning and Placement Center. Ask yourself what factors make you a unique applicant and expand those categories. Any product has to have unique marketable characteristics.

RELATE PAST EXPERIENCE AND FUTURE PLANS
TO THE POSITION

Try to show how your work/life experience has prepared you for this specific position and how it would move you toward your future goals and objectives. Explain why you and the position seem perfect for each other.

AVOID BEING NEGATIVE

Be careful not to project any insecurity you may feel about your qualifications. Either in writing or verbally, do not dwell on your shortcomings or those of others with whom or for whom you have worked. Do not offer negative information. Be honest about answers, but not blunt. Honesty involves factually answering questions, bluntness involves volunteering negative information the interviewer may or may not want to hear. Answer questions by trying to include information that also points to your strengths, achievements, qualifications, and goals.

CHAPTER 7

Coming to Closure in the Job Hunt

Blue and Gold, 1891

EVALUATING A JOB OFFER

If successful in convincing an employer to hire you, you usually can expect a written or verbal offer within two to three weeks, although some employers may take either much less or much more time to make a decision. Some employers, when extending an offer of employment, require an acceptance or rejection by a given date, usually a week to ten days after the offer date. Other employers leave their offers open-ended, requesting that you notify them as soon as you have made a decision.

When an employer sets a deadline which you find is too limited, request an extension of time in which to consider the offer—an additional week or two is usually considered reasonable. Immediately recontact employers in whom you still have an interest, and from whom you have had no response. Inquire as to your current status with that organization and explain that you have received an offer and need to make an employment decision soon. Such an inquiry may prompt some employers to expedite the decision process. Other employers may be unable to do so, and you will then have to decide whether you should take a certain offer or risk waiting for another, perhaps better, offer.

The selection criteria that you developed with your statement of career objective would be helpful to consult when you are trying to evaluate a job offer. Does the job have all of the "musts" you deemed necessary? Which "wants" does it include? Consult Chapter Two to refresh your memory, if necessary.

In considering the pros and cons of a job, the decision you make today is not necessarily the decision you will have to live with for the rest of your life. Most people change careers several times in their lifetime. What is more important for your first position is your ability to get along well with your co-workers and learn. With whom will you be working? Will you enjoy the work? Will it provide a challenge? Will it provide you with the training and experience necessary for promotion to positions compatible with your goals? Salary, as long as it is in the range of current offers for similar positions, may be a secondary consideration. Acceptance of an employment offer should be made in good faith and with sincere intention to honor the commitment. Do not accept an offer before you are ready. It is neither ethical nor in your best interest to accept a job and then a week or two later tell the employer: "Sorry, I received a better offer." Employers need a firm commitment on your part in order to plan their staffing needs. It is also unethical to accept a "career" job that involves extensive training if your plans include returning to graduate school a few months later.

After reaching a final decision, write your letter of acceptance or your letter of regret. In letters of acceptance, be sure to include your understanding of the job title, salary, location, moving expenses, starting date and any other contractual arrangements that may have been discussed.

DETERMINING SALARY

It is important that you understand the specifics of your salary and benefits when accepting a position. Employers generally discuss salaries when they are interested in offering you a job. If the employer has not specified a salary figure at the time the offer is made, it is appropriate to inquire. It is best not to begin discussion of salaries at the first interview. Ideally, this subject should be brought up by the employer. The keys to successfully arriving at a salary mutually agreeable to you and the employer are:

1. Know Yourself and Your Needs. List all your anticipated monthly expenses. Be sure to include transportation, new wardrobe, change in rent, professional memberships, etc. Check the cost of living in the area where you will reside. Refer back to the analysis you did in Chapter Two about your financial needs. Re-establish the minimum salary which you would be willing to accept and the salary you think is necessary to meet all essential living expenses.

2. Research Current Salaries and Benefits. It is important to be aware of the current salary range for the position you are seeking. To research current salaries in your field of interest, review recent past job listings and salary information at your nearest career library, consult the *College Placement Council Salary Survey*, and talk with your career planning and placement advisor. Understand that in addition to salary, compensation may include benefits such as health and dental insurance, sick and vacation leave, as well as profit sharing. Remember, benefits increase your earnings—especially where profit sharing or bonuses are involved. Many employers have regularly scheduled salary increases, commissions and bonuses, educational reimbursements, travel expenses, etc.—be sure you are aware of these.

3. Discuss Your Salary Expectations. If the salary and benefit package offered does not meet your personal needs or is not competitive with similar positions you have researched, you may politely explain this to the employer and ask that the offer be reviewed. Be sure to clearly state your reasons. Most employers have a salary range in mind and many are not allowed to negotiate a salary once a specific figure has been offered. Try to determine from the employer what the range is and exactly how they arrived at the offer. Once you understand the assumptions and calculations that were made, you are better able to negotiate the offer.

THE TRANSITION FROM STUDENT TO EMPLOYEE

Expectations created during the job search are not always fulfilled when you start a new job. The job may have sounded very glamorous during the interview process because you wanted it to sound fantastic or perhaps the interviewer might have been overzealous in presenting the position to gain and hold your interest. Regardless of your expectations, you should now focus on making the most of your new position. At the same time, your employer will probably be most concerned about seeing that you can handle your new responsibilities competently.

The New Job

Some of the strategies used to help new employees become functioning and productive staff members include:

On-the-Job Training. Performing the regular assignments under the supervision of experienced staff members (including your supervisor) who are available to lend additional support as needed.

Rotational Training Programs which provide training on short-term job assignments in different units or divisions of the organization while working full-time. Normally these temporary working periods are three to twelve months in duration. Evaluations may be made of your progress at the end of each assignment.

Formal Classroom Training may be interspersed with on-the-job training or rotational programs in order to supplement and speed up the learning process. In some instances, this formal training may be done as the first step in integrating the new employee into the work environment.

The "Sink or Swim" Approach leaves you completely on your own with some responsibility but an unclear job assignment with little guidance from senior staff. Under this circumstance, it is advisable to seek clarification of your responsibilities and additional feedback as to how you are doing.

No matter what approach is taken in your training, you should make it a point to seek out a mentor who is interested in and willing to help you. A mentor is a more experienced person who works in your organization and is friendly enough to answer your questions from time to time. Mentors are useful for discussing your work problems and obtaining advice on how you can best approach those problems. Mentors can also help you learn what others do in the organization and how their jobs relate to yours. They will be valuable for finding needed information at later times.

ORGANIZATIONAL REALITIES

Try to understand the "big picture" as to how the organization works, its purpose, and whom it serves. Be sensitive to the work culture, namely, what behavior is acceptable and unacceptable, how people relate to one another, and what behavior is most rewarded. Often new college graduates are eager to try to make changes. Before proposing changes try to understand why things are the way they are—how the current way of doing things came to be, what benefits that way of doing things has, and who in the organization is strongly committed to the current way.

RELATIONSHIPS WITH OTHERS

Most workplaces have a "pecking order," and as the newest hire you are apt to be near the bottom. This may involve doing certain tasks that are not of interest to you or taking work direction from someone you may not particularly like. You will probably work with many different types of people in terms of age, education, experience, values and opinions. You may even find your position somewhat lonely in that there may not be many others of your own age. To combat this, try extending yourself to your fellow workers using the job as a mutual focus of interest. Do not be afraid to ask someone to join you for lunch or to introduce yourself to people in other departments.

Learning to deal effectively with your supervisor is very important. Become familiar with his or her style of dealing with subordinates. Be sure to understand what is expected of you in terms of work assignments, communication, and handling problems. Your supervisor is your most important link to the rest of the organization—be sure it is a strong connection!

YOUR PERSONAL WORK STYLE

If you have not already, you might want to give some thought to how you work best in a work environment. Are you good at setting your own work pace? How independently do you like to work? Do you prefer special projects or work where responsibilities remain constant? By being aware of what you need to do your best work, you can communicate your preferences in the workplace.

COMMUNICATING AT WORK

Communication is the exchange of information in a manner that is mutually understood. Communication can be written, oral, or non-verbal.

Being skilled at all forms of communication is necessary to be effective at work. When communication breaks down, as it often does, some of the variables that inhibit clear communication are:

☐ incomplete information

☐ oral information when written is more appropriate, such as in complex instructions, exact deadlines, etc.

☐ written information when oral would be more appropriate, such as in showing the importance of a certain task

☐ information to or from the inappropriate person

☐ information at an inappropriate time

☐ improper use of language, the choice of words and what they convey.

Some of these barriers can be broken down by using some of the following techniques:

☐ actively listening, that is, showing that you understand what is being said and where unsure, repeating the information back to the other person

☐ listening for emotional content as well as informational content

☐ obtaining feedback to be sure that others understand what you are trying to communicate

☐ being attentive to non-verbal cues such as facial expressions, tones of voice, eye contact, and body movements.

THE INTANGIBLES OF GETTING ALONG ON THE JOB

In the work environment there are many factors that affect how one gets along on the job that are never stated but are clearly understood by most employees. People often refer to these factors as the work norms of the organization. Sometimes the processes of the organization take on a political tone, as different personalities maneuver to each gain additional resources. You should avoid becoming involved in such conflicts while you are still new to the organization, but be aware that they exist. Watch for special interest groups, elements of both formal and especially informal power, external constituencies important to the organization, participation in organization-sponsored events, and elements of organizational protocol.

YOUR EARLY CAREER YEARS

Research on the topic of careers has shown that during the early years of a career the employee is:

☐ developing expertise to lay groundwork for promotion or lateral career growth

☐ developing creativity and motivation

☐ becoming an effective and contributing member of the organization

☐ developing a sense of personal values and direction

☐ learning what work is really like

☐ balancing demands of work with the pursuit of other interests

☐ balancing the need for independence with organizational restrictions and requirements during a period of subordination and dependence

☐ deciding whether to remain in the organization or occupation or to seek new opportunities.

GETTING AHEAD ON THE JOB

Probably key to your success in your position is demonstrating a high level of competence in your area of responsibility. With that as a given, there are still several barriers that can keep you from being perceived as being effective. These perceptions can actually influence your ability to be effective, as others act based upon their perceptions. Below are the most common roadblocks you should be aware of:

☐ inability to get along with others

☐ minimal, baseline performance of job duties

☐ avoiding responsibility and/or new or different responsibilities

☐ becoming very routine about work

☐ being negative and closed to change, finding reasons for not doing things

☐ inability to handle constructive criticism

☐ attitude that you are above the job, are working too hard, or are underpaid

☐ seeming to be insensitive to the "political" factors of the organization.

ENHANCING YOUR CAREER DEVELOPMENT

Career development is a lifelong process. It is in your hands, not those for whom you work. The first job is not the end of your career planning but the beginning of a new cycle of your career. Your organization may have career development or human resources specialists on its staff. Getting to know these individuals and discussing your career interests with the right people at work can be enormously helpful in planning and realizing your future development. Often career planning is an official part of your supervisor's responsibilities. Hopefully, he or she will be able to provide you with excellent guidance and support, if you take the initiative to seek them. Let your supervisor know your interests on an ongoing basis; do not wait for an annual review. Take advantage of in-house and external learning opportunities. Be aware of both horizontal and vertical opportunities within your organization and chances to do special projects that would enhance your skills and your value to the organization.

CHAPTER 8

Special Topics and Resources

Blue and Gold, 1881

WORKING IN BUSINESS
WITH A LIBERAL ARTS DEGREE

Although this book is not necessarily directed toward liberal arts majors going into business, liberal arts graduates are becoming more interested in business as a career direction. Many of these students believe that the only way to get a job in business is to major in business administration and then interview with employers when they come on campus. Such students are misled by three assumptions. The first is that "business" endeavors are clearly defined. They are not. Any endeavor undertaken for profit qualifies as "business." The second assumption concerns the role of the business administration major. This major does not qualify the student for ANY position. He may be less qualified than the liberal arts major for positions requiring qualitative skills such as personnel or public relations. The third assumption is that the business administration major always obtains his job through on-campus interviewing. This assumption is also false. Like any other major, he may also obtain his job through friends, family, faculty, direct job listings, want ads and his own job search. Like any other major, he does his share of informational interviewing and library research.

So ... like any business major, the first place for you to start if you are interested in working in business is to identify what areas of business interest you. There are many opportunities in any business, each of which differs widely in tasks performed and skills and qualifications required. You must be specific in identifying your objective when applying to work in any business. It is not enough to say that you are interested in management or in a management trainee program, for example. Few, if any, new college graduates are initially qualified for a position as a manager, yet almost any position they might take could lead to managerial responsibilities involving resources, dollars, and people. Any initial position would also develop the skills of planning, organizing, implementing, and controlling—all of which are essential management skills. Once employed, you may take advantage of formal and "on the job" training. Employers are educators; in fact, employers now spend more money for educational and training programs than is spent by all U.S. colleges and universities combined.

Most businesses have in common four specific organizational areas:

☐ Sales/Marketing
☐ Administration
☐ Production/Manufacturing
☐ Finance

Most entry-level opportunities for liberal arts students are commonly found in the first two.

Positions in sales/marketing include such activities as market research, advertising and sales, which exist to identify customer needs, research new product markets, establish sales goals, develop advertising campaigns, and directly sell the product.

Individuals in administration are responsible for providing legal, personnel, labor relations, and public relations support for the production, finance, and marketing areas. These individuals maintain positive internal and external relations among management, employees, government, and the public.

Employees in production/manufacturing research, design, develop, produce, and distribute the product or service sold to customers. These employees are usually technical personnel, such as researchers, engineers, quality control and transportation specialists.

Financial analysts summarize the financial position of a business for top decision makers. These analysts develop systems and procedures for gathering, processing, and analyzing data on income and expenses. They analyze potential investments, prepare budgets and economic forecasts. They may also audit company accounts to determine if projects remain within budget limitations as well as prepare data for tax computation. Individuals working in finance usually have very strong analytical skills and have usually received a bachelor's or master's degree in finance, accounting, mathematics, computer science, or economics.

SAYING YOU WANT TO GO INTO BUSINESS DOESN'T MEAN MUCH ... WHICH ASPECTS?

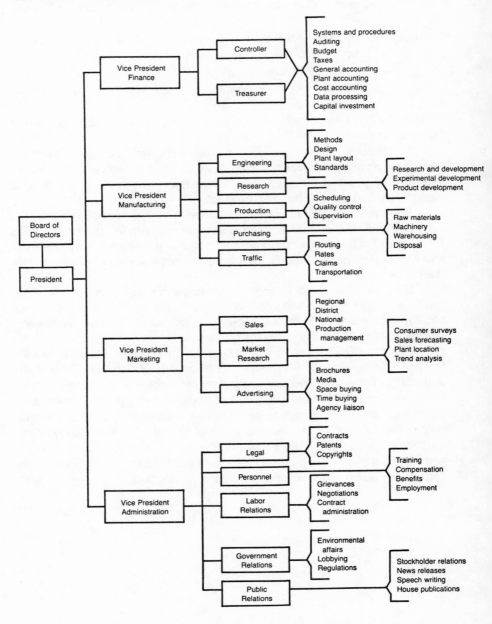

C. Randall Powell, *Career Planning Today*. Dubuque, IA: Kendall/Hunt Publishing Company, 1981. Used by permission of Kendall/Hunt Publishing Company.

Typical Entry-Level Opportunities

SALES

Although the role of the sales representative is regarded with ambivalence by many liberal arts students, the unfavorable image of sales people is largely incorrect. Alert, ethical sales representatives are needed to "educate" increasingly sophisticated customers about increasingly sophisticated products. In short, they are needed to sell understanding. For the liberal arts student interested in business, sales offers positions with great opportunity to learn about the company's products and services. Good sales people are always in demand, so plenty of opportunities exist which tend to have high compensation and opportunity for advancement. Successful sales representatives must often be willing to work long hours, be independent, and endure the economic uncertainty of compensation partially or entirely through commissions on sales.

Marketing research and sales are not synonymous. Marketing researchers analyze data about potential sales markets, often in order to predict the sales volume of a product or service. It usually is necessary to have a degree in a quantitative field which includes statistics to compete successfully for professional marketing jobs. Sales is a function which is specifically established to generate purchases from new and existing customers for the company's products or services. Successful sales representatives must have the intelligence and flexibility to constantly learn new information and techniques; the perseverance and self-discipline to organize their time; and the self-confidence and communication skills to approach strangers and handle frequent rejection or to work effectively with an established client anticipating needs and ensuring good service.

Many businesses will start sales representative trainees with a base, or guaranteed, salary plus a commission on sales. Often after a stipulated training period the trainee is gradually shifted to strictly commission, depending on the company and the product being sold. Sales representatives can choose to remain in direct sales or move into sales training and supervision. Those who remain in direct sales often handle larger and more complex sales of sophisticated products to larger accounts. Sales trainers and supervisors recruit and train new sales representatives and motivate and evaluate the performance of the sales force.

Another common route into sales supervision for recent graduates is through retail store supervision. Retail store supervisors plan and evaluate the work of sales clerks and other employees, and often arrange sales displays. Retail store supervisors can be promoted to buyer positions, purchasing wholesale merchandise for resale. Such positions may offer extensive travel opportunities. Experienced sales representatives with approximately five to seven years of experience may move into management, to help identify new customer markets and their product needs.

SALES SUPPORT POSITIONS

After a sales representative has completed a sale, a variety of workers help insure that the product or service is delivered and operating properly. For example, a computer operator trainer will teach the customer's employees how to use newly purchased computer equipment. An account executive for a copy machine distributor visits current customers to see that the machines are meeting the customer's needs. Insurance claims adjusters will investigate losses suffered by a policy holder to determine how much should be paid on a claim. An underwriter reviews an insurance contract to determine if the potential policy holder is paying adequate premiums to cover the risk to be assumed by the insurance company. Workers in these jobs need the tact to deal with complaining customers and the patience to be good teachers.

PERSONNEL

Often those liberal arts majors who want to work with people will consider working in personnel as their career objective. The assumption, however, that all personnel workers work strictly with people is inaccurate. Personnel practitioners do not work with people any more than employees in other occupations. In fact, workers in some personnel specialties have relatively little involvement with other people.

Personnel practitioners are involved with programs concerning the recruitment, selection, training, retention, compensation and safety of employees. Their objective is the most effective utilization of the company's human resource. Their objective is not simply to help people per se. The activities of personnel practitioners are listed below, in an approximate descending order of the amount of interpersonal contact in each activity.

Recruiting. Duties include advertising open positions, interviewing applicants, negotiating compensation offers, monitoring Equal Employment Opportunity compliance.

Training. Duties include designing and conducting programs to teach workers how to perform their duties, or to teach supervisors how to maintain the productivity of their subordinates.

Occupational Health and Safety. Duties include careful review of provisions of OSHA (Occupational Safety and Health Act), inspecting the workplace for compliance, or arranging for outside consultants to make the inspection, and writing detailed reports.

Labor Relations. Duties include negotiating contracts and resolving disputes between employers and employees. To enter this field, you usually need considerable experience in the other personnel activities, so there are not many entry-level positions.

Compensation Analyst. Duties include conducting detailed statistical studies of prevailing levels of wages and fringe benefits paid to various worker groups, and writing detailed reports on the findings.

Personnel practitioners may be generalists or specialists. Generalists are proficient in most or all of the areas of personnel activity. Specialists concentrate in one of the areas. Recent graduates usually begin in one of the less technical activities, such as recruiting. They then develop into generalists after two to three years and may become specialists in another five or so years. Experienced personnel practitioners may supervise the work of subordinates, and advise top decision makers in a business about human resources legislation and policies. While the ability to work well with people is important, other skills, such as the ability to communicate effectively, are equally important.

ADVERTISING

Advertising and public relations are fields that tend to have a reputation for creativity and variety. As a result, there are always many applicants for whatever opportunities are available. These opportunities tend to be more numerous in the cities of New York, Chicago, and Los Angeles, where most of the major advertising firms are headquartered.

Advertising is used to motivate customers to buy products. Common jobs in advertising include:

Copy Writer Writing the words, or copy, which appear in ads and sales newsletters. Copy writers may write scripts for advertisements for television or radio.

Layout Artist Combining copy with visual artwork to create a pleasing, attention-grabbing arrangement.

Account Executive Account executives consult with marketing researchers to study the client's sales, public relations and advertising problems and goals. From these variables advertising campaign strategies are planned. Account executives then coordinate the activities of copywriters and layout artists to create advertising to meet their customer's demands. Copy writers, layout artists or advertising sales representatives can progress to this position. Account executives can be promoted to handle larger and more complex accounts, or they may eventually open their own agencies.

Successful applicants for positions in advertising usually have talent in writing, commercial art, and/or selling. They tend to thrive in a highly varied, creative, competitive, pressure-filled environment.

PUBLIC RELATIONS

Public relations, like advertising, is generally known as a "glamour field." Many applicants compete for relatively few job openings. Public relations practitioners promote good will, develop credibility, and create a favorable public image for their employers. They extol the benefits of their employer's product or service to various publics, such as: the media, customers, stockholders, regulatory agencies, as well as the general public. Public relations practitioners may specialize in governmental affairs or lobbying with public officials. Work in public relations involves a great deal of writing. They write press releases, magazine articles, and speeches. They must also be adept public speakers themselves.

One way to enter the field of public relations is through reporting for small local newspapers, called "shoppers," then possibly working for a large company on the "in-house" public relations staff. An experienced individual may manage an in-house public relations group or move to an outside public relations agency that works with many companies. After many years of experience and a sizable clientele, an individual could do consulting or open his or her own firm.

OPERATIONS

Employees in operations supervise and coordinate the activities of other workers, often clerical, to keep the day-to-day activities of a business going. Operations supervisors study production schedules and estimate worker-hour requirements for completion of assignments. They analyze and resolve work problems, and motivate and/or discipline subordinates. For example, operations managers in banks supervise tellers and clerks in their daily activities. In a public utility, a customer service manager supervises workers who resolve customer complaints. Employers either hire recent graduates as operations supervisors directly, or "bring them through the ranks" of clerical or paraprofessional workers. Operations managers need to be able to identify the causes of work problems, be objective enough to divorce personalities from other potential causes of problems, and be tactful enough to correct the performance of subordinates.

ALTERNATIVES TO TRADITIONAL EMPLOYMENT

Most of the discussion in this book has been aimed at locating a full-time position in an organization. There are other viable alternatives that graduates select every year that are not so traditional in nature. Here are two important ones that you too might want to consider:

Working for Yourself

Many individuals have a dream of working for themselves in a business they have created. Many people plan such opportunities for retirement, but some start building such an opportunity as soon as they graduate. The advantages of working for yourself are clear to most people: independence, flexibility, control are some of the most commonly cited attractions in being your own boss.

To increase the chances of success, many individuals go into business with others. For example, someone who recently graduated from college might team together with a professional who is already successful in the field. By doing this, you gain the advantage of someone who is experienced in the field and who has an extensive network of contacts. Likewise, joining with other students who share common interests can help to minimize your total costs while at the same time sharing experiences, resources, and business contacts that are made.

Work Time Options

More and more people are considering alternatives to a full-time work schedule. Two work time options which are becoming increasingly well accepted are permanent part-time employment and job sharing. Permanent part-time employment is work that is less than full-time but has a career orientation and prospects for upward mobility. Job sharing is when two people share the responsibilities of one full-time position with salary and fringe benefits prorated.

These options are pursued by people who for a variety of reasons may want to work at one job less than the full-time standard of 40 hours per week. It has special advantages for those who may be attending graduate or professional school or raising small children. From the employer's point of view, the main advantage of job sharing appears to be that two people can bring to a job different talents, different perspectives, and make the job even stronger. More information on work time options can be requested from New Ways to Work, a non-profit work resource and research organization based in San Francisco.

APPENDIX **A**

Finding a Summer Job

Blue and Gold, 1879

SUMMER JOBS IN BUSINESS

No matter what your major is, there is a broad range of jobs in business available for you to consider. Typical employers would include:

Accounting. Manufacturing companies, fast food chains, restaurants, hotels, electronics firms, transportation companies, food processing companies, computer services companies, state and federal governments and banks. Many small companies use students for data entry positions. Be sure you mention computer experience on your resume.

Economic Analysis and Policy. Transportation companies, public utilities, economic modeling firms.

Finance. Banks, chemical processing companies, U.S. government.

Management Science and Production Management. Manufacturing companies, insurance companies, banks, food processing companies, aerospace firms, consulting.

Marketing. Manufacturing companies, management companies, insurance companies, business machine companies, computer service companies, transportation companies, pharmaceutical companies, food distributing companies, retail.

Organizational Behavior and Industrial Relations. Banks, federal government, retail, financial services, manufacturing.

Real Estate and Urban Land Economics. Banks, brokers, syndicates.

Typical summer jobs would include:

Accounting. Accounting intern with a corporation or accounting firm, budget analyst, financial auditor, general voucher reconciliation, and cost accounting analysis.

Economic Analysis and Policy. Assist in developing econometric models, economic specialist for regulatory affairs.

Finance. Budget analyst, lending or operations trainee, cash management analyst, consolidation reporting financial management intern.

Management Science and Production Management. Systems and procedures assistant, insurance operations trainee, operations management and credit function interns, administrative intern, production coordinator.

Marketing. Customer service, sales support, leasing sales trainee, marketing service, account executive, casualty/property claims and commercial lines, market survey research, campus representative, route sales representative, purchasing assistant.

Organizational Behavior and Industrial Relations. Personnel research assistant, personnel management intern.

Real Estate and Urban Land Economics. Marketing/sales, appraisal.

Do you want to work in business but don't know how to begin? Do you wonder what type of job a liberal arts/social science major might find in the business community? The following "first" experiences which other students had in a business setting may give you some ideas for your summer job search. Make an attempt to explore jobs that are related to your major or tentative career interests.

BA Math. Worked part-time and summers for a record company. Was hired as a fill-in typist, but was promoted to Assistant to Office Manager, managing accounts payable.

BA Economics/Environmental Studies. Worked two summers for an instrumentation firm as a Shipping-Receiving Clerk. Was responsible for stockroom inventory, receiving purchased goods and maintaining all records.

BS Economics. Part-time and summers as a Campus Representative for a large textbook wholesaler. Organized and managed book exhibitions for faculty of various departments.

BA Psychology. Assistant Office Supervisor in warehouse. Handled customer problems, ordered warehouse stock, kept inventory, supervised employees.

BS Business Administration. Worked with a helicopter manufacturer and assisted in the project proposal for submission to the federal government.

BA Classical Languages. Worked for gift shop specializing in art objects and jewelry. In addition to being sales clerk, executed cash and lay-away sales transactions. Prepared bank deposits. Reconciled cash receipts with recorded data. Was promoted to Assistant Manager with responsibility for training and supervising workers.

BA History. Conducted a survey of newspaper readership patterns, including statistical analysis, for a local newspaper.

BA Journalism. Public Relations Intern for a meat-packing firm. Wrote articles and took photographs for company magazine. Wrote and designed booklets, posters and displays.

SUMMER JOBS IN GOVERNMENT

The Federal Government offers summer opportunities that are advertised initially in December in Announcement 414—*Summer Jobs in the Federal Government*, available through your career planning placement center or your regional branch of the U.S. Office of Personnel Management. The categories of employment, listed with the level of government pay scales in parentheses, include:

GROUP I

For undergraduates (GS-1 through GS-4). These jobs, primarily clerical, are located in federal agencies nationwide, mainly in urban areas. Opportunities are limited and therefore highly competitive.

GROUP II

Direct application, undergrads. The jobs in this group are technical and non-clerical (GS-1 through GS-4). Opportunities for summer employment in each of the agencies listed are extremely limited when compared to the large number of applicants. Students are advised to apply as soon as information becomes available in late November. Agencies in this group include:

- ☐ Environmental Protection Agency
- ☐ U.S. Geological Survey
- ☐ Consumer Product Safety Commission
- ☐ Department of Defense-Civil Preparedness Agency
- ☐ Department of Treasury-Internal Revenue Service
- ☐ Veterans Administration Hospitals

GROUP III

A limited number of job opportunities involving professional and administrative work (grades GS-5 and above) will be available in this group. To be considered for summer employment in this group you must be a college graduate (June graduating senior), a graduate student planning on attending graduate school, or a faculty member. Deadlines vary from agency to agency.

Other summer opportunities exist in the government through special programs that vary from year to year. Examples are:

Student Trainee. Students in this program participate in specific training programs during vacations and attend college full-time during the academic year. Students selected under this program receive career appointments and are promoted to professional positions upon graduation. Deadlines are generally in April.

Legislative Assistant. For those students interested in working in a congressional office during the summer, a number of representatives and senators hire students to do constituent casework, research legislation, and to write press releases. Because there is no established program, availability of internships and application procedures varies from office to office. Generally, these internships are voluntary and non-paid. Students are advised to check with individual representatives or senators to see if they are interested in sponsoring an intern. Two excellent resources for locating and identifying these potential sponsors are the latest copies of the Congressional Membership Directory and the Directory of the Committees of the Congress (both available at most libraries).

Other agencies such as the U.S. Department of State, Federal Trade Commission, National Endowment for the Arts, and the Agency for International Development and the Organization of American States conduct summer internships that are not announced in the Federal Summer Announcement. You might have to specifically check with each of these agencies as well as state and local government agencies that might offer summer employment opportunities for students.

SUMMER JOBS IN ENGINEERING, COMPUTER SCIENCE AND PHYSICAL SCIENCE

If you are interested in summer work in these fields, use the information below for examples of typical summer work assignments and major employer types.

Engineering

MECHANICAL ENGINEERING

Examples of typical summer work assignments: Work in a research group assembling model prototypes; performance testing and preparing engineering calculations; preparation of computer input for a piping systems analysis program; refinery work; assist in feasibility studies of alternative forms of energy; assist with equipment design.

Some major types of employers: Equipment manufacturers; electronics, petroleum, and construction industries; aerospace industries; public utilities; consulting firms (hire primarily graduate students).

CIVIL ENGINEERING

Examples of typical summer work assignments: Various duties related to water utilities; surveying and drafting; routine pavement design tests and product evaluation work; blueprint review and calculations; on-site construction work; transportation.

Some major types of employers: Federal Government, State and local governments; public utilities; construction firms; contractors; consulting firms (hire primarily graduate students).

ELECTRICAL ENGINEERING

Examples of typical summer work assignments: Electronic schematic drafting and printed circuit layout; electronic equipment testing; circuit design layout and testing; design; quality assurance; research and development.

Some major types of employers: Electronics firms (both instrument manufacturers and semiconductor firms); public utilities; computer manufacturers; aerospace firms; research laboratories.

CHEMICAL ENGINEERING

Examples of typical summer work assignments: Assist in chemical research lab in a consumer products division; research assistance in nuclear firm; process development and fermentation work; refinery work.

Some major types of employers: Petroleum, chemical, construction industries; electronics firms (especially semiconductor firms); consulting firms (especially environmental consulting firms—hire mostly graduate students).

INDUSTRIAL ENGINEERING

Examples of typical summer work assignments: Analyze procedures and systems in manufacturing or public utilities; time and motion studies; test experimental equipment and process control; methods improvement, standards, packaging, warehousing and distribution in food processing or chemical manufacturing.

Some major types of employers: Manufacturing industries: processing industries (e.g., food, paper, or chemicals); public utilities; health delivery facilities; Federal Government agencies.

MATERIALS SCIENCE

Examples of typical summer work assignments: Test and process technicians.

Some major types of employers: Electronics, aerospace, research labs, Federal Government, utilities.

NUCLEAR ENGINEERING

Examples of typical summer work assignments: Power, nuclear research.

Some major types of employers: Federal Government, utilities, research labs.

COMPUTER SCIENCE

Examples of typical summer work assignments: Opportunities available in both scientific and business applications (programming, documentation, flow charting, coding and some software development).

Some major types of employers: Computer manufacturers, computing services (which develop programs for specific applications), electronics firms, aerospace firms, utilities, research labs, banks.

Physical Science

PHYSICS

Examples of typical summer work assignments: Process technicians (semiconductor and computer firms), test technicians, lab technicians (field measurements), scanner.

Some major types of employers: Electronics firms, aerospace firms, research labs, computer manufacturers.

CHEMISTRY

Examples of typical summer work assignments: Lab technician (instrumental analysis, quantitative analysis, defect analysis, organic synthesis), process test technician, quality control technician.

Some major types of employers: Chemical firms, oil companies, research labs, electronic firms, food industry, environmental consulting firms.

MATHEMATICS/STATISTICS

Examples of typical summer work assignments: Computer programming, marketing (computers), test monitoring, quality assurance technicians, research assistants.

Some major types of employers: Electronic firms, aerospace firms, computer manufacturers, research labs, computer services firms, insurance companies (benefits clerk), utilities, State Government.

GEOLOGY/GEOPHYSICS

Examples of typical summer work assignments: Field exploration, lab assistants, research assistants.

Some major types of employers: Oil companies, construction firms, consulting engineering firms, mining firms, Federal Government (e.g. U.S. Geological Survey), State Government.

SUMMER JOBS OUTDOORS

If you want to work outside during the summer, here are several places to consider:

U.S. Forest Service—hires in the areas of Forestry, Biological Science, Range, Survey and Engineering.

National Park Service—hires park aides, technicians and rangers.

Bureau of Land Management—hires in the areas of fire control, forestry, resources conservation, recreation, engineering, surveying and physical sciences.

U.S. Fish and Wildlife Service—hires students with strong fish and/or wildlife biology background to assist in these areas.

Youth Conservation Corps—hires college students to coordinate their high-school-age conservation camps. The camps are run on public lands by the Forest Service, National Park Service, Bureau of Reclamation, and other agencies. Students may apply to as many camps as they wish. Funding for this program is at times tenuous, so interested students should make appropriate confirmations.

U.S. Geological Survey—hires a limited number of students majoring in geology, geophysics, hydrology, mining, and/or petroleum engineering.

EIP (Environmental Intern Program)—hires for paid internships with government, private industry or non-profit organizations. There are currently four programs located in: California, Pacific Northwest, Lower Great Lakes, and the Northeast. Persons who have completed three years of college are eligible to apply.

In addition, many jobs are available through private companies, such as concessionaires, operating in the National Parks. Also consider contacting the Student Conservation Association, Box 550, Charlestown, NH 03603, which is a non-profit organization placing students as park and forest assistants in the national parks and forests leading hikes, giving camp fire programs and other visitor-related activities. Positions are volunteer, but all living and travel expenses are paid.

SUMMER JOBS ABROAD

Jobs overseas are not numerous and in most cases will cost you more than you can expect to earn. Each country has laws regarding visas and work permits; most are for three to six months. Longer permits are typically more difficult to obtain. Recommended reading for anyone interested in employment abroad for the summer is a pamphlet entitled "A Word of Caution" put out by the U.S. Department of State. Most of the jobs, which are primarily found in Europe, fall into one of the following categories:

Short-term unskilled—includes food service workers, resort workers, and camp counselors. Employers generally require that you speak the language of the host country. Many programs obtain a short-term work permit for you and assist you with leads for obtaining a job when you arrive in the country. A few programs will place you in a job prior to your arrival.

Au pair—living with and working for a family. Positions are available in a number of countries.

Work camps/service programs—these are generally volunteer. You may expect room, board, and the satisfaction of helping others. Jobs often involve hard, physical labor, such as helping build a school or repair a road. Sometimes jobs are found working in social service agencies. Archaeological digs are also found in this category.

Trainee programs/internships—short-term skilled jobs. Generally, the student is paid enough to cover living expenses. Many of these programs are on an exchange basis and require a specific skill and at least two years of college. Well known examples are IAESTE, an exchange program for students in technical fields, and AIESEC, an exchange program for students in the field of international business. Your career planning and placement library will most likely have the most current addresses for these programs.

You can find out information about most of the programs listed in this Appendix, as well as state and local programs, in your campus career planning and placement center. If you do not find it there, check in the reference section of your public library.

APPENDIX *B*

Bibliography of Employer Information Sources

Blue and Gold, 1899

INTRODUCTION AND GENERAL REFERENCE TOOLS

In today's job market it is usually necessary to seek out employers rather than wait for them to come to you. It is also useful to know as much as possible about an organization before you approach it regarding employment. This bibliography, *Employer Information Sources in Print*, is designed to help you use your Career Planning and Placement Center Library and to be aware of other campus libraries which collect information about employers. It will be most helpful to you if you *have a career field in mind* and need information about people or organizations to whom you might apply for jobs, and/or want to know more about a specific employer before you make contact or go for an interview.

Most of the books included in this bibliography are directories. They often list organizations by career fields and/or geographic area. They include the names and addresses of professional associations and trade journals as well.

Most directories are arranged so that you can locate an entry in them if you

☐ know the name of an organization,

☐ are interested only in organizations in one *geographic area,*

☐ are interested in organizations which carry a particular *product* or offer a particular *service.*

Directories have several limitations:

1. They are *out of date as soon as they are published*, because organizations and their officers change continually.
2. There is *no guarantee about a specific item's currency or accuracy.* It is a good idea to check addresses and names in current telephone books before contacting a listed group.
3. Directories *rarely cover all organizations connected with a field.* They usually focus on a type of employer or a geographical area. To be thorough, you will need to consult several directories.

Current directories of employers are usually kept in the Reference Collection of a library, but they are not always entitled "Directory of ..."

Other title words which often indicate a book that may be useful as a directory of employers are: "Buyer's Guide to ...", "Yearbook of ...", and "International Almanac".

GENERAL REFERENCE TOOLS

Each of the directories listed in this section provides information about organizations, activities, and people in more than one career or subject field. You will find included everything from directories of volunteer organizations and professional associations to lists of alternative career opportunities, research centers, and sources of grant funding. It will be useful to scan the entries in this section no matter what your career interest is.

Telephone books may also serve as directories of employers. Your university or public libraries usually have extensive collections from cities around the country. Other materials you may wish to use in gathering information about employers are:

> Directories of Associations
> Directories of Directories
> Directories of Foundations and Grants
> Directories of Periodicals
> Specialized Periodical Indexes

Some subject headings which can be used to locate these and other related materials are:

> Associations and Societies—Directories
> Endowments—Directories
> Research—United States—Directories
> United States—Directories

NOTE: Don't hesitate to ask a library staff member to help you locate the books listed in the next pages or other materials on careers that interest you.

GENERAL DIRECTORIES

Following is a list of directories found in most career libraries:

Annual Register of Grant Support, 1982–83. Chicago: Marquis Professional Publications, 1983.

Lists many government agencies, public and private foundations, businesses, and professional associations in the U.S. and abroad which offer grants to individuals and groups. Includes information on objectives of various programs, types of support available, application information, typical numbers of applicants and awards.

Career Employment Opportunities Directory, Vol. I, Liberal Arts and Social Sciences. Santa Monica, CA: Ready Reference Press, 1980.

Lists career employment opportunities for Liberal Arts and Social Sciences majors offered by numerous businesses, government agencies, and professional organizations nationwide. Organized alphabetically by organization name.

✓ *Career Opportunity Index for California.* Semi-annual with bi-weekly updates, 1984.

Both editions of this magazine, the Professional Edition and the Vocational Technical Edition, list current openings for which businesses in California are recruiting. There is also a section which has detailed profiles of these employers.

College Placement Annual. Bethlehem, PA: College Placement Council, 1984, Annual.

An annual publication containing a brief description of many employers in business, industry and government and their major recruiting needs.

✓ *Consultants and Consulting Organizations*, ed. by Paul Wasserman. Detroit: Gale Research, 1984.

Facts about more than 5,000 firms and individuals serving as consultants for business and industry.

Directory of Career Training and Development Programs. Santa Monica, CA: Ready Reference Press, 1979.

A comprehensive guide to career training and development opportunities available from business, government and professional organizations. Includes management development programs, operations development programs, field sales training programs, and special development programs.

Directory of College Recruiting Personnel—1984. Bethlehem, PA: College Placement Council, Inc., 1984.

Lists organizations that recruit on college campuses nationwide. Includes organization name, address, nature of business, number of employees. Provides names and titles of key college relations and recruiting personnel and location information where different from headquarters.

Directory of Directories, published by Information Enterprises, distributed by Gale Research Co., 1982.

Subject areas include: business, agriculture, law, science, education, social sciences and humanities, arts, public affairs, health, etc.

Directory of Internships, Work Experience Programs and On-the-Job Training Opportunities, ed. by Alvin Renetzky. Thousand Oaks, CA: Ready Reference Press, 1976.

Lists opportunities available from government, business and industry, professional associations, social and community organizations in the United States. Organized alphabetically by program title; provides subject and geographic indexes.

First Supplement to Directory of Internships, Work Experience Programs, and On-the-Job Training Opportunities, 1978.

Directory of Undergraduate Internships, ed. by Debra L. Mann and Grace E. Hooper. Washington, D.C.: National Society for Internships and Experiential Education, 1982.

Lists nationwide internship opportunities, including information about program design, requirements, remuneration and academic credit.

Franchise Opportunities Handbook. Washington, D.C.: U.S. Department of Commerce, 1983.

Lists equal opportunity franchisers who set requirements on the availability, terms or conditions of their franchises. Provides a brief summary of the terms, requirements, and conditions under which the franchises are available. Includes general information on franchising, suggestions, and checklists to assist and protect the potential investor.

The Future: A Guide to Information Sources. Washington, D.C.: World Future Society, 1979.

Contains a wide range of information sources now available in the field of futuristics. Resources include individuals, organizations, research projects, books, reports, periodicals, films, audiotapes and tape series, games and simulations, media presentations and courses offered by educational institutions. Also features a glossary of terms frequently found in writing about the future.

Information Industry Market Place. New York: R.R. Bowker Company, 1984.

Describes the range of information products available, includes the subject coverage, currency, access method, and scope of services. Organized alphabetically in seven major sections and eighteen subsections.

International Directory of Little Magazines and Small Presses. Paradise, CA: Dustbooks, 1982.

Alphabetical listing of publishers of little magazines and small presses. Gives addresses, titles of publications, costs, average press runs, etc.

Internship Programs in the West: Review and Catalog. Boulder, CO: Western Interstate Commission for Higher Education, 1981.

Provides profiles of internship education activities in the Western U.S. Includes 593 "academic" and "professional" programs, indexed by key words.

National Directory of Addresses and Telephone Numbers. New York: Bantam Books, 1983.

Lists 50,000 organization addresses and telephone numbers. Includes sections as follows: Business and Finance; Professional Business Services; Government, Politics & Diplomacy; Education, Foundations, Religious Denominations, Hospitals, Hotlines & Social Services; Associations and Unions; Transportation and Hotels; Communications & Media; Culture & Recreation; Business Services.

1982 & 1983 National Directory of Addresses and Telephone Numbers. Haverford, PA: Haverford College Career Planning Office, 1983.

Sectioned by career field, lists name of sponsoring organization, addresses and contact person. Contains a description of each internship, its duration, hours per week, salary/stipend, academic credit, and requirements.

Research Centers Directory. Detroit: Gale Research, 1983, with supplements.

Lists groups conducting research in many fields from education and life sciences to business and law. Describes the centers in fair amount of detail. Useful for those interested in doing research work.

Toll-Free Digest. Claverack, NY: Toll Free Digest Co., 1983.

Lists over 25,000 toll-free telephone numbers.

Training and Development Organizations Directory, ed. by Paul Wasserman and Marlene A. Palmer. Detroit: Gale Research, 1983.

Reference work describing firms, institutes, and other agencies offering training programs for business, industry and government. Contains alphabetic, geographic, broad subject, subject and alphabetical list of individual indexes.

1983 Yellow Pages of Employers. Gaithersburg, MD: Prospect Press, 1983.

Provides names and addresses of over 1,000 employers who have recently advertised for professionals in specific disciplines as well as interdisciplinary fields. Disciplines covered are: business, education, engineering, life sciences, social and behavioral sciences, and physical sciences. Arranged alphabetically by employer name. Contains an index by discipline.

DIRECTORIES OF ASSOCIATIONS

Directories listed below can help you identify associations connected with your career field, the journals and newsletters they publish, and where to write for more information about meetings and local branches.

Career Guide to Professional Associations: A Directory of Organizations by Occupational Field. Cranston, RI: The Carroll Press, 1980.

This directory is organized by occupational fields; gives names of associations and addresses. Also includes a "comment column" telling about organizational publications, if any, educational aids, employment assistance, etc. particular to each professional association.

Encyclopedia of Associations, Detroit: Gale Research, 1984. With supplements, 5 Vols.

Volume I "National Organizations of the U.S." covers a wide range including business, science, legal, education, cultural, social welfare, health and public affairs.

Volume II "Geographic and Executive Index"—U.S., Canada and Foreign.

Volume III "New Associations and Projects"—quarterly supplements.

Volume IV "International Organizations."

Volume V "Research Activities and Funding Programs."

National Trade and Professional Associations of the United States. Washington, D.C.: Columbia Books, 1984 (annual).

Overlaps with above directory in some ways, but often provides different information. Information about headquarters, chief officers, activities and publications is usually given. Key word and geographic indexes make it easier to find associations connected with a given field or based in a certain geographical area.

BUSINESS & INDUSTRY

This bibliography is organized into the following subsections:

General

Directories of Specific Industries

Don't hesitate to ask a library staff member for assistance when you are looking for the books on this list or for other related materials.

The *subject headings* to check in a library card catalog to find these and similar materials include:

Advertising—Direcs.

Banks and banking—Direcs.

Big Business—Direcs.

Commerce—Direcs.

Corporations—U.S.—Direcs.

Elec. data processing—Yearbooks

Manufacturers—Direcs.

Marketing—Direcs.

Use the *periodical indexes* to find current articles on specific employers or listings of specialized directories, e.g.:

Business Index (available on microfilm)

Business Periodicals Index

Predicasts F & S Index, United States, Europe, and International

Public Affairs Information Service

Wall Street Journal Index

Following is a list of business and industrial employer directories available in most career libraries.

GENERAL

"California's Leading Companies—1983," reprinted from the Business Section, *Los Angeles Times*, May 15, 1983.

Lists largest companies which have headquarters in California and publicly held stock. Companies are ranked by sales/revenues for year-end 1982 or fiscal year 3/31/83.

"The Fortune Directory of the Largest U.S. Industrial Corporations." New York: *Fortune Magazine*, May 3, 1982.

Lists the 500 largest industrial corporations in the U.S. and ranks them by sales. Includes their assets, net income and stockholders' equity.

"The Fortune Directory of the Largest U.S. Non-Industrial Corporations." New York: *Fortune Magazine*, June 13, 1983.

Lists company rankings for the 100 largest diversified financial, diversified service, and commercial banking firms. Lists company rankings of the 50 largest life insurance, retailing, transportation, and utility companies. Companies are ranked by sales, and listings include assets, net income, and stockholders' equity.

Career Guide to Professional Associations: A Directory of Organizations by Occupational Field. Cranston, RI: The Carroll Press, 1980.

Organized by occupational fields, gives names of associations and addresses. Also includes a "comment column," telling about organizational publications, if any, educational aids, employment assistance, etc. particular to each professional association.

✓ *Consultants and Consulting Organizations Directory*, ed. by Paul Wasserman. Detroit: Gale Research, 1984.

Facts about more than 5,000 firms and individuals performing consulting work in a variety of fields.

Management Consulting '84. Boston, MA: Harvard Business School, 1984.

Provides information about 48 business management consulting firms. Provides recruiting contact's name and title, organization name, address and phone number.

National Directory of Corporate Public Affairs, 1984. Washington, D.C.: Columbia Books, Inc., 1984.

Provides a profile of the corporate public affairs profession in the U.S.—identifying the key people and principal corporate offices from which the many forms of public affairs activities are conducted.

Standard and Poor's Register of Corporations, Directors and Executives. New York: Standard and Poor, 1984, vols. I, II, III.

Volume I contains corporate listings in alphabetical sequence. Entries include addresses, names, titles and functions of key people; annual sales; division names and functions; subsidiary listings. Volume II contains individual listings of directors and executives in alphabetical sequence. Volume III contains 6 indexes: Standard Industrial Classifications, Standard Industrial Classification Codes, Geographic, Obituary, New Individuals Additions, New Company Additions.

Top 200 Corporations in the United States. Sausalito, CA: James R. Albin, 1978.

Directory of "top 10% of publicly held companies in the United States." Contains information about each company such as: net income, net sales, shareholders equity, etc.; gives names of directors, executive officers, transfer agents, etc.

Trade and Professional Associations in California: A Directory. Claremont, CA: California Institute of Public Affairs, 1982.

Lists non-profit business and professional associations in California. Chambers of Commerce are not included. Arranged alphabetically by organization name. Indexed by subject.

Walker's Manual of Western Corporations. Long Beach, CA: Walker's Manual, Inc., 1984.

Two-volume set including alphabetic corporate index, advertiser index, patron companies index, list of OTC margin stocks, geographic index, classification index. Each entry contains: company address, market, business, and extensive income and expense statistics.

Who's Who in Training and Development. Baltimore, MD: ASTD Publishing Services, 1983.

Provides complete list of members of the American Society for Training and Development. Contains index of members listed by organization name. Includes index of members by region and chapter, and women's network members.

DIRECTORIES OF SPECIFIC INDUSTRIES

American Bank Directory. Norcross, GA: McFadden Business Publications, 1983.

Contains an alphabetical list of all banks in the United States including national, state, savings and private banks arranged in state order, indicating the names of officers, directors and principal correspondents.

The National Directory of Certified Public Accountants and Accounting Firms. Princeton, NJ: Peter Norback Publishing Co., 1981.

This nationwide directory lists certified public accountants, accounting firms, schools and professional associations.

O'Dwyer's Directory of Public Relations Firms—1984. New York: J. R. O'Dwyer Co., Inc., 1984.

Lists major U.S. public relations firms. Contains indexes by specialization, geography, advertisers by type of service, and others.

Packaging Marketplace. Detroit, MI: Gale Research Company, 1978.

A directory of materials and services in the packaging field, divided into the headings, "Information", "Services", "Materials", and "Equipment". Under each heading, the entries are arranged by geographical locations. Each entry provides address, telephone number and executive officer.

1983 Sportsguide. Princeton, NJ: Sportsguide, Inc., 1983.

Lists national and regional organizations including trade show directories, business and consumer media, editorial and advertising sources, trade associations officials and promotion, executives who are active in the sports field.

Standard Directory of Advertisers. Skokie, IL: National Register Publishing, 1983, with supplements through 1984.

Provides classified subject and alphabetical access to over 17,000 companies doing national or regional advertising. A directory of large American companies, their products, and the media and agencies they use for advertising.

Standard Directory of Advertising Agencies. Skokie, IL: National Register Publishing, February, 1980.

A roster of major ad agencies and their branches. States names of chief personnel and major accounts the firms handle.

1984 U.S.A. Oil Industry Directory. Tulsa, OK: Penn Well Books, 1984.

Lists principal oil companies in the United States. Divided into sections as follows: integrated oil companies, large independent producers, drilling fund companies, pipeline transmission, marketing firms, associations, and government agencies.

World Aviation Directory. New York: Ziff-Davis Publishing, 1983 Annual.

Lists aviation/aerospace companies and officials in the U.S., Canada, 164 countries in Europe, Central and South America, Africa, the Middle East, Australia, and Asia.

COMMUNICATION, MEDIA, ARTS

This bibliography is organized into the following sub-sections:

> General
> Publishing, Writing
> Photography, Film and Broadcast Media
> Libraries
> Museums and Historical Societies
> Design, Illustration and Fine Arts
> Performing Arts and Music

Some subject headings to check in the library card catalogs to locate more information about employers in the Communication, Media and Arts fields include:

> Art—Direcs.
> Art—U.S.—Direcs.
> Libraries—Direcs.
> Museums—Direcs.
> Photography—Direcs.
> Publishers & Publishing—Direcs.
> Television—Direcs.
> Theater—Direcs.

Use the *periodical indexes* to find current articles on employers and for listings of more specialized directories, e.g.:

Art Index
Library Literature
Public Affairs Information Service

Following is a list of directories available in most career libraries. For international communication, media, and arts directories, see section entitled "International".

GENERAL

Arts Yellow Pages. New York, NY: Associated Council of the Arts, 1977.

Contains listings for various governmental, U.S. and Canadian arts agencies, arts advocacy groups, arts centers, national arts publications, etc. Lists addresses, phone numbers and possible contact people.

Careers in the Arts: A Resource Guide. New York, NY: Center for Arts Information, Opportunity Resources for the Arts, 1981.

Identifies the books, organizations, and other resources in the arts. Contains sections on performing arts, visual arts and crafts, film/video/audio, museums, humanities, literature, and the arts administration. Includes internship and apprenticeship information in each field.

The Workbook: California Edition, Vols. I, II. Hollywood, CA: Scott and Daughter Publishing, 1984.

Lists a variety of California firms of interest to fine, commercial, and performing artists. Includes advertising agencies, department stores, magazines, film studios, record companies, radio stations, design studios, production artists, photographers, artists' representatives, and commercial production companies. A second volume contains information about portfolio suppliers.

PUBLISHING, WRITING

American Book Trade Directory. New York, NY: R. R. Bowker, 1983.

Lists book retailers, antiquarians, and wholesalers of books and magazines in the U.S. and Canada. Includes book trade information: auctioneers, appraisers of literature, foreign language book dealers, export and import firms, etc. Also contains publishers in the U.S. and Canada.

1983 Ayer Directory of Publications, pub. by William J. Leudke. Philadelphia: Ayer Press, 1983.

The professional's directory of print media published in the U.S., Puerto Rico, Virgin Islands, Canada, Bahamas, Bermuda, Republic of Panama, and the Philippines. Economic descriptions of states, cities, etc. in which listees are published. Includes 69 custom maps on which towns and cities of publication are indicated.

The Directory of Publishing Opportunities in Journals and Periodicals. Chicago, IL: Marquis Academic Media, 1981.

Describes subject interests, editorial policies and manuscript requirements for over 3,400 scholarly and trade journals in humanities, social sciences, sciences and industrial and professional fields. Useful directory of places to publish reports on research or general scholarly essays.

International Directory of Little Magazines and Small Presses. Paradise, CA: Dustbooks, 1983.

Three basic kinds of listings: magazines (periodicals), presses (book publishers) and cross references.

Journalism Career and Scholarship Guide 1981. Princeton, NJ: The Newspaper Fund, 1981.

Provides career information about the field of journalism. Includes lists of schools which offer accreditation and scholarship information.

Literary Market Place. New York, NY: R. R. Bowker, 1983.

A directory of book, magazine and newspaper publishers; writing and publishing associations; literary agents and agencies; translators; and radio and TV programs featuring books. Useful for writers, illustrators, or photographers interested in working on a freelance or regular basis in the writing and publishing industry.

MIMP 1984: Magazine Industry Market Place. Ann Arbor, MI: R. R. Bowker, 1984.

Lists magazines, journals and other periodical publications and their publishers. Includes advertising and public relations agencies, professional associations, editorial services, printers and others.

1983 Writer's Market: Where to Sell Your Work, by P. J. Schemenaur. Cincinnati, OH: Writer's Digest, 1983.

Notes on how to go about being a freelance writer supplement the listings of magazines, publishers, literary agents, play producers and other buyers of a writer's work. Lengthy descriptions about the subject interests and manuscript handling practices are included with each entry.

PHOTOGRAPHY, FILM, AND BROADCAST MEDIA

(AVMP) Audio Visual Market Place: A Multimedia Guide. New York, NY: R. R. Bowker, 1983.

Lists producers and distributors of non-print media as well as professional associations, festivals and equipment suppliers.

Film Etc.: Historic Preservation and Related Subjects, compiled by Don Lippman. Washington, D.C.: The Preservation Press of the National Trust for Historic Preservation, 1979.

Lists alphabetically 16 mm color sound films for general adult audiences on historic preservation and related subjects.

International Motion Picture Almanac. New York, NY: Quigley Publishing, 1984.

A directory of film makers, distributors, movie equipment suppliers, and other groups involved in many aspects of the production and distribution of movies.

International Television Almanac. New York, NY: Quigley Publishing, 1984.

Provides addresses, names of personnel, and program specialties for major TV producers, program distributors, networks and stations as well as companies involved in support services such as animation, equipment or special effects.

Photographer's Market. Cincinnati, OH: Writer's Digest Books, 1984.

Lists a variety of employment sources for photographers. Organized by organization type, includes contact name and title. Also contains general career information for photographers.

The Production Company LA. Beverly Hills, CA: Parmorand Publications, 1982.

Lists Los Angeles area motion picture and television production companies alphabetically by firm name.

The Student Guide to Mass Media Internships (1982). Eau Claire, WI: Dept. of Journalism—University of Wisconsin, 1982.

Lists information about training programs for students in mass media organizations, Organized alphabetically by state, city, and organization name.

LIBRARIES

American Library Directory. New York, NY: R. R. Bowker, 1983.

Lists libraries in the U.S., Canada, Puerto Rico, and regions administered by the U.S. Includes sections on library systems; libraries for blind and physically disabled persons; networks, consortia and other library organizations; state school library agencies; library schools and training courses.

California Library Directory, 1983, ed. by Coleen Clark. Sacramento, CA: Library Services Bureau, 1983.

Begins with a section of information about the California State Library, the California Library Services Board, cooperative public library systems, and public library address list. The directory section lists libraries alphabetically by name. Includes information about population served and whether or not open to public.

Special Libraries Association 1981–82 Membership Directory—San Francisco Bay Region Chapter. Burlingame, CA: American Library Association, 1981.

This publication lists names, addresses and telephone numbers of chapter members and sustaining members; also provides a list of special libraries in alphabetical order, as well as indexes by subject and location.

MUSEUMS AND HISTORICAL SOCIETIES

Directories of Historic Preservation Organizations Outside the United States. Washington, D.C.: The Preservation Press, Nat'l Trust for Historic Preservation in the U.S., 1978.

Lists a wide variety of historic preservation organizations worldwide. Organized alphabetically by name of country.

Directory of Historical Societies and Agencies in the United States and Canada. Nashville, TN: American Association for States and Local History, 1982.

Descriptive register of historical commissions, archive and history departments, state and local historical associations. Lists staff size, major programs, and subject focus of collections.

The Official Museum Directory, Skokie, IL: National Register Publishing, 1984.

Lists museums in the United States and Canada. Organized first by state, then city within state alphabetically. Also indexes museums alphabetically by name and discipline; includes a listing of principal personnel at each institution.

Directory of Private, Nonprofit Preservation Organizations: State and Local Levels. Washington, D.C.: Preservation Press, Nat'l Trust for Historic Preservation, 1980.

Lists historic preservation organizations alphabetically by state and city.

DESIGN, ILLUSTRATION AND FINE ARTS

American Art Directory, 1982. New York, NY: R. R. Bowker Co., 1982.

This volume is divided into three major categories: art organizations, art schools, art information. Also included is a personnel index containing position and location of each person involved in one of the three sections.

Artist's Market: Where to Sell Your Commercial Art. Cincinnati, OH: Writer's Digest, 1983.

Lists firms that hire artists. Organized alphabetically by employer type. Includes names and titles of key staff, type of artwork used and application information.

PERFORMING ARTS, MUSIC

Music Industry Directory. Chicago, IL: Marquis Professional Publications, 1983.

Contains listings for service and professional organizations, schools and colleges, periodicals, festivals, competitions, foundations and music businesses.

The Songwriter's Handbook, by Harvey Rachlin. New York, NY: Funk and Wagnalls, 1977.

Covers writing and marketing songs. Includes brief directories of music associations, professional organizations, licensing organizations, music publishers and record companies.

TCG Theater Directory 1983–1984. New York, NY: Theatre Communications Group, Inc., 1983.

Contains contact information for the theaters comprising Theatre Communications Group. Provides nationwide listings alphabetically arranged by theater name.

Theatre Profiles/5. New York, NY: Theatre Communications Group, 1982.

Describes in detail the activities, philosophy, and repertoire of about 100 non-profit professional theater groups in the U.S.

GOVERNMENT, LAW, PUBLIC ADMINISTRATION

Most libraries have the *basic* federal and state government directories.
The entries in this section are grouped into these sub-sections:

> General Government
> Federal Government
> State Government
> Law and Law Related

Some *subject headings* to check to find materials on government careers, paralegal work, public and social administration include:

> Lawyers—Direcs.
> Lawyers—U.S.—Direcs.
> State Governments—Yearbooks
> U.S.—Politics & Government—handbooks, manuals, etc.

Use the periodical indexes to find current articles on specific employers or listings of specialized directories, e.g.:

> Monthly Catalog of Government Publications
> Public Affairs Information Service

GENERAL GOVERNMENT

Directory of Public Service Internships. Washington, D.C.: National Society for Internships and Experiential Education, 1981.

A guide to internship and fellowship opportunities nationwide. Entries include information about program objectives and design, selection procedures, and requirements.

Directory of Washington Internships. Washington, D.C.: National Society for Internships and Experiential Education, 1983.

Lists internship opportunities in the nation's capital. The entries are divided into general fields of interest and include the organization's or sponsoring agency's name, address, phone number, and contact person.

Federal, State, Local Government Directory, Vols. I, II. Washington, D.C.: Braddock, 1981.

Provides names, addresses and phone numbers of official staff in the White House, Executive Dept., Independent Agencies and Commissions, Regulatory Agencies, Legislative and Judicial branches of the U.S. Government. Lists National and State political committee officers, chief state and local government officials and state/local government organizations nationwide.

Washington Information Directory, 1982–83. Washington, D.C.: Congressional Quarterly, 1982.

Lists agencies of the executive branch of the federal government, Congress, and non-profit (non-governmental) organizations. Contains subject index.

FEDERAL

Congressional Staff Directory, ed. by Charles B. Brownson. Mt. Vernon, VA: Congressional Staff Directory, Ltd., 1983.

Lists congressional staff; includes State Delegates, U.S. Senate, Joint Committees, Library of Congress, U.S. House of Representatives, key personnel of the Executive Office, and independent agencies.

Congressional Yellow Book. Washington, D.C.: The Washington Monitor, 1984.

A comprehensive guide to the people and committees in the federal government: senators and aides, representatives and aides, senate committee aides, house committee aides, joint committee aides and miscellaneous.

Federal Government Legal Career Opportunities. Chicago, IL: American Bar Association, 1976.

A thorough guide to employment in the federal government for lawyers; includes employment statistics, selection factors, location of employment, nature of legal work, opportunities for promotion, and how to apply.

Federal Regulatory Directory, ed. by Robert E. Healy. Washington, D.C.: Congressional Quarterly Inc., 1983.

Lists every agency with rule-making powers. Introduces the reader to the topic of regulation and provides in-depth profiles of major regulatory agencies, including key contacts, informational sources, organizations, and regional office locations.

Federal Yellow Book. Washington, D.C.: The Washington Monitor, 1983.

A loose-leaf directory of the federal departments and agencies of the United States government; provides addresses and phone numbers.

1981–82 Student Work-Study Programs with Federal Agencies. U.S. Office of Personnel Management, Western Region, 1981.

Part I describes various programs and special appointing authorities agencies use to employ students. Part II provides a listing of Federal Agency Work-Study Coordinators in the Western Region.

U.S. Government Career Brochures.

Leaflets that describe career opportunities and/or agencies.

United States Government Manual. Washington, D.C.: U.S. National Archives and Records Service, General Services Administration, 1983.

Describes the purposes and programs of most federal government agencies and lists the top personnel. Includes brief statements about some commissions and international organizations.

Washington Representatives, 1984. Washington, D.C.: Columbia Books, 1984.

This directory contains names, addresses, and phone numbers of Washington lobbyists, consultants, registered foreign agents, legal advisors, public relations and governmental affairs representatives. In many cases, organizational representatives are noted.

Washington '84. Washington, D.C.: Columbia Books, Inc., 1983.

Listing of officials in the three branches of federal government, newspapers, radio and television stations, foreign media, press clubs, cultural institutions, savings and loan banks, national associations, etc. Almost all entries are in the Washington, D.C., area.

STATE GOVERNMENT

State Information Book. Washington, D.C.: Potomac Books, 1982.

Entries are organized by state and contain lists of major state services, state legislatures, courts, and federal agency branches. Entries provide addresses and telephone numbers.

LAW AND LAW RELATED

Martindale-Hubbell Law Directory. Summit, NJ: Martindale-Hubbell, 1984, Annual, 7 vols.

The standard guide to attorneys and law firms. Provides brief descriptions about each lawyer's background and the firm's practice. Also includes a law digest.

HEALTH, EDUCATION, WELFARE

This bibliography is organized into the following sub-sections:

> Education (Teaching and Administration)
> Health and Social Science

Some *subject headings* to check in the library card catalogs to locate more information about employers in the Health, Education and Welfare fields include:

> Aged—Societies & Clubs—Direcs
> Education—Direcs
> Handicapped child—Educ—Direcs
> Hospitals, Convalescent—Direcs
> Psychiatric clinics—Direcs
> Public Schools—U.S.—Direcs
> Public Welfare—U.S.—Direcs
> Universities & Colleges—Direcs
> Universities & Colleges—Direcs

Use the *periodical indexes* to find the most current information on employers and names of more specialized directories, e.g.:

> *Education Index*
> *Psychological Abstracts*
> *Public Affairs Information Service*

Following is a list of directories available in most career libraries:

EDUCATION (TEACHING AND ADMINISTRATION)

Directory of Career Planning and Placement Offices 1983–84. Bethlehem, PA: College Placement Council, 1984.

Lists name and location of college, the name, title, and telephone number of the career planning and placement director. Organized alphabetically by state.

Education Directory: Public School Systems in the U.S. WI: ASCUS Publications, 1983.

State certification offices and interstate agreements on credentials in addition to school district addresses listed alphabetically by state.

The Handbook of Private Schools. Boston, MA: Porter Sargent, 1983, Annual.

A compendium of information about day and boarding schools in the U.S. and Canada.

Information on Colleges and Universities, 1983–84. Pittsburgh, PA: United States Steel Corp., 1983.

Lists colleges and universities nationwide. Includes names and titles of academic staff in engineering and business departments and placement center directors.

The ISS Directory of Overseas Schools 1983/84. Princeton, NJ: International Schools Services, 1983.

This directory lists more than 350 schools worldwide. International Schools Services is a recruiting service for overseas education and also operates some schools under contract with companies. Gives brief information on countries and some cities.

Schools Abroad of Interest to Americans. Boston, MA: Porter Sargent, 1982.

Describes private elementary and secondary schools situated outside the continental United States. Includes schools' locations, program offerings, number and international composition of faculty and enrollment.

Teachers' Guide to Overseas Teaching, by Louis A. Bajkai. La Jolla, CA: 1983.

A complete and comprehensive directory of English-language schools and colleges overseas. Indexed alphabetically by country.

Teaching Abroad. New York, NY: Institute of International Education, 1984.

Lists and describes organizations and sponsors conducting teaching-abroad programs for U.S. elementary, secondary, adult education, college-level teachers, guidance counselors, and administrative personnel.

HEALTH AND SOCIAL SERVICES

Good Works: A Guide to Social Change Careers, ed. by Karen Ciptaken. Washington, D.C.: Center for Study of Responsive Law, 1982.

Provides profiles of people engaged in full-time citizen work. Lists related organizations and provides a compilation of resources and networks. Included is a description by each organization of their goals, projects, and staff needs.

Medical and Health Information Directory, ed. by Anthony T. Kruzas. Detroit: Gale Research Co., 1980.

Guide to state, national, and international organizations including government agencies, educational institutions, hospitals, grant award sources, journals, and research centers.

Mental Health Services Information and Referral Directory: Eastern and Western Regions. Thousand Oaks, CA: Specialized Indexes, Inc., 1978.

This two-volume directory contains sections providing a guide to regional services arranged in alphabetical order by state and by city; sections providing mental health statistics; and sections listing mental health resource information. Each entry includes: address, telephone number, geographic areas served, auspices, services provided.

National Health Directory. Washington, D.C.: John T. Grupenhoff, 1984.

Comprehensive list of more than 7500 key information sources on health programs and legislators including names, addresses, and telephone numbers. Listed are key personnel of federal agencies now moving to regulate health-medical affairs; information officers for every HEW program; major health committees; Congressional representatives with their health legislative aides and appointment secretaries in Washington D.C. Includes state legislators, state health agencies and their key officers.

Public Welfare Directory. Chicago, IL: American Public Welfare Association, 1983.

Lists and describes the programs of federal, state, and local government agencies in the U.S. and Canada that offer social services.

Social and Behavioral Sciences Jobs Handbook: The Insider's Guide for Specialists in Society and Human Behavior. Gaithersburg, MD: Prospect Press, 1982.

Lists a wide variety of employers who have indicated an interest in hiring social science majors. Also contains position descriptions, related fields, and professional alternatives, nationwide job listing sources and employment information.

Social Service Organizations and Agencies Directory, ed. by Anthony T. Kruzas. Detroit, MI: Gale Research Co., 1982.

Includes non-profit associations, advocacy groups, professional societies and local, state, and federal government agencies. Classified by area of service; agencies are listed alphabetically.

INTERNATIONAL

Books listed in this section cover employers in any and all career fields. Although some of the books include United States references, their primary focus is international.

The entries in the following pages have been grouped into these subsections:

General
Business and Industry
Communication, Media, Arts
Health, Education, Welfare
Science

The basic *subject heading patterns* to use in locating international directories in a library's card catalog are:

☐ The name of a country or continent followed by the word "Directories" or "Yearbooks", e.g., "Great Britain—Directories"; "Africa—Yearbooks".

☐ The name of a career field followed by the name of a country or continent followed by the words "Directories" or "Yearbooks", e.g., "Art—Europe—Directories".

Use the periodical indexes to find current articles on specific employers and listings of specialized directories, e.g.:

Predicasts F & S Index, Europe and International Public Affairs Information Service

NOTE: If you are interested in *working in Canada*, also investigate the books listed in the various other sections of *Employer Information Sources in Print*. Although not always indicated in the titles, many of these books cover Canada as well as the U.S.

Foreign embassies and consulates often have information about organizations and job opportunities in their countries. A list of their addresses appears in *Europa Yearbook.*

Following is a list of directories available in most career libraries:

GENERAL

Careers in International Affairs. Washington, D.C.: School of Foreign Service, Georgetown University, 1982.

Includes overseas employer listings, with addresses, for the United States government, public international organizations, international banking and business, international consulting firms, research organizations, teaching, national trade and professional associations, trade unions, assistance, exchange, foundations and other non-profit organizations, press, radio and television.

Directory of European Associations, 2 vols. Detroit, MI: Gale Research Co., and Beckenham Kent, U.K.: CBD Research, Ltd. Part I: 1981, Part II: 1984.

Lists over 9,000 European organizations in English, French, German. Part I includes national industrial, trade and professional associations. Part II lists national "learned", scientific and technical societies.

Guide to Careers in World Affairs. New York, NY: Foreign Policy Association, 1982.

Lists a small sample of sources of employment in four areas: international employment, non-profit and non-governmental, international business, government and the United Nations.

International Directory for Youth Internships. New York, NY: U.N. Headquarters, NGO Youth Caucus, 1977–78.

This directory of intern and volunteer opportunities includes a country-by-country listing of field offices, non-governmental organizations, world federation of the United Nations Associations' National Committees, general information on employment opportunities within the United Nations.

International Foundation Directory, ed. by H. V. Hodson. Detroit, MI: Gale Research Co., 1984.

Lists worldwide philanthropic organizations involved in research and education. Organized alphabetically by country.

National Trade and Professional Associations—Labor Unions of the U.S. and Canada. Washington, D.C.: Columbia Books, Inc., 1984.

Lists approximately 6,000 national trade associations, labor unions, scientific or technical societies, and other national organizations composed of groups united for a common purpose.

Overseas Summer Jobs. Cincinnati, OH: Writer's Digest Books, 1983.

Organized alphabetically by name of country, lists types of work and contact information.

Summer Jobs Britain 1984, ed. by Susan Griffith. Oxford, United Kingdom: Vacation Work, 1981.

Provides information that will assist students in finding summer jobs in England, Scotland and Wales. Includes list of firms that welcome applicants from outside of Britain. Contains visa and work permit requirements which they must fulfill.

Work, Study, Travel Abroad: Whole World Handbook, by Marjorie A. Cohen. New York: Council on International Education Exchange, 1984.

A student's guide to work, study and travel abroad. Although opportunities for study are the emphasis, sources of employment information are also listed.

BUSINESS & INDUSTRY

American Register of Exporters and Importers. New York, NY: American Register of Exporters and Importers, 1979.

Includes alphabetical list of American Chambers of Commerce abroad, indexes of products, advertisers. Main register lists organizations alphabetically by product and name, also includes addresses.

Directory of American Firms Operating in Foreign Countries, Vols. I, II, III. New York, NY: Uniworld Business Publications, 1984.

Volume I provides an alphabetical index including telephone numbers, addresses, major officers, numbers of employees, products, and foreign office locations. Volumes II and III provide alphabetical distributions of the firms by country.

"The Fortune Directory of the Largest Industrial Corporations Outside the United States". New York, NY: *Fortune Magazine*, August 23, 1982.

Lists the 500 largest foreign industrial corporations and ranks by sales. Includes their assets, net income, stockholders, equity and number of employees.

World Aviation Directory. New York, NY: Ziff Davis Publishing Co., 1983.

Lists aviation/aerospace companies and officials in the U.S., Canada, 164 countries in Europe, Central and South America, Africa, the Middle East, Australasia and Asia.

International Directory of Little Magazines and Small Presses. Paradise, CA: Dustbooks, 1983.

Lists magazines and presses worldwide. Includes names of magazines, presses, editors, addresses, phone numbers, types of material published and comments by editors.

COMMUNICATION, MEDIA, ARTS

International Motion Picture Almanac, ed. by Richard Gertner. New York, NY: Quigley Publishing, 1984.

A directory of film makers, distributors, movie equipment suppliers and other groups involved in many aspects of the production and distribution of movies.

International Television Almanac, ed. by Richard Gertner. New York, NY: Quigley Publishing, 1984.

Provides addresses, names of personnel, and program specialties for major TV producers, program distributors, networks and stations as well as companies involved in support services such as animation, equipment or special effects. Despite the name, it focusses on the U.S.

Translation and Translators: An International Directory and Guide, ed. by Stefan Congrat-Butler. New York, NY: R. R. Bowker Co., 1979.

Includes translators' associations, centers, awards, fellowships, grants, prizes, model contracts, copyright, register of translators and interpreters , translators' marketplace. Also lists legislation, journals, books, recent history and breakthroughs in the translation field.

HEALTH, EDUCATION, WELFARE

The ISS Directory of Overseas Schools 1983/84. Princeton, NJ: International Schools Services, 1983.

This directory lists more than 350 schools worldwide. International Schools Services is a recruiting service for overseas education and also operates some schools under contract with companies. Gives brief information on country and some cities.

Invest Yourself. New York, NY: The Commission on Voluntary Service and Action, 1982.

A catalog of paid and volunteer opportunities with voluntary service groups in North America and abroad. Includes community service, institutional and individual service openings with local government agencies, recreation programs, youth hostels, VISTA alternative schools, etc.

Schools Abroad of Interest to Americans. Boston: Porter Sargent, 1982.

Describes private elementary and secondary schools situated outside the continental United States. Includes schools' locations, program offerings, number and international composition of faculty and enrollment.

Teachers' Guide to Overseas Teaching, by Louis A. Bajkai. La Jolla, CA, 1983.

A complete and comprehensive directory of English-language schools and colleges overseas.

Teaching Abroad. New York, NY: Institute of International Education, 1984.

Lists and describes organizations and sponsors conducting teaching-abroad programs for U.S. elementary, secondary, adult education, college-level teachers, guidance counselors and administrative personnel.

SCIENCE

Worldwide Directory of National Earth-Science Agencies and Related International Organizations. Washington, D.C.: U.S. Dept. of the Interior, 1981.

Provides addresses of governmental earth-science agencies around the world that have functions similar to the U.S. Geological Survey. Also lists addresses of major international organizations that are concerned with some phase of the earth sciences. Arranged alphabetically by name of country.

RECREATION & TRAVEL

This bibliography is organized into one general section that lists recreation and travel directories. Performing Arts careers are covered in the section "Communication, Media, Arts". For directories pertaining to foreign employment, see "international" sections.

Some *subject headings* to check in the card catalog for other materials on careers in these fields include:

> Airlines—Timetables
>
> Camps—U.S.—Direcs.
>
> Hotels, taverns, etc.—U.S.—Direcs.
>
> The name of a city, region, or state followed by "—Directories"; e.g., "San Francisco—Directories"

Use the *periodical indexes* to find current articles on employers and listings of specialized directories, e.g.,

> Public Affairs Information Service

NOTE: The *best directories of employers in these career fields* are often hotel, restaurant, and business guides published by a chamber of commerce, travel guide books, and local telephone directories.

Following is a list of directories available in most career libraries.

GENERAL

Buyers Guide and Camp Directory, 1981. Huntington, NY: Camp Consulting Services, Ltd., 1981.

The Buyers Guide section catalogs companies which provide services to camp owners/directors nationally and internationally. Suppliers are listed alphabetically with a classified index of the products and services available. The Camp Directory lists American and international camps, summer programs and organizations alphabetically. Provides information for both summer and winter. Includes clientele types and program descriptions. Contains geographic index.

National Recreational, Sporting & Hobby Organizations of the U.S. Washington, D.C.: Columbia Books, Inc., 1983.

Lists approximately 2,800 national organizations serving the recreational and avocational interests of Americans. Organized alphabetically; indexed geographically and by subject heading.

Parents' Guide to Accredited Camps. Martinsville, IN: American Camping Association, 1983.

Lists general and special camps accredited by the A.C.A. Provides names of directors, addresses, dates of sessions, types of facilities, and descriptions of special clienteles or programs organized by camp type.

Recreation and Outdoor Life Directory, ed. by Paul and Steven R. Wasserman. Detroit, MI: Gale Research Co., 1983.

A guide to national, international, state and regional organizations, federal grant sources, foundations, consultants, special libraries, and information centers, research centers, educational programs, journals and periodicals and state and federal leisure activity facilities.

1983 Sportsguide. Princeton, NJ: Sportsguide, Inc., 1983.

Lists national and regional organizations including trade show directories, business and consumer media, editorial and advertising sources, trade association officials and promotion executives who are active in the sports field.

Summer 1982, Directory of Summer Opportunities. Andover, MA: A.I.C., Inc., 1982.

Lists colleges within the United States and overseas offering many different summer academic enrichment and/or basic skills programs. Includes information about camp jobs, government jobs, summer internships, travel and a variety of other valuable summer educational and employment opportunities.

1981 Summer Employment Directory of the United States. Cincinnati, OH: Writer's Digest Books, 1983.

Contains state-by-state listings of job openings in the U.S.—in Canada, and 164 countries in Europe, Central and South America, Africa, the Middle East, Australasia and Asia.

SCIENCE, ENGINEERING AND ENVIRONMENTAL DESIGN

This bibliography is organized into the following subsections:

General
Chemistry and Physics
Computer Science
Energy and Environmental Protection
Engineering
Environmental Design
Life Science

Some *subject headings* to check in the card catalog to locate similar materials include:

> Agricultural Research—U.S.—Direcs.
> Architects—U.S.—Direcs.
> Biological Laboratories—U.S.—Direcs.
> Cities and Towns—Planning—Direcs.
> City Planners—U.S.—Direcs.
> Laboratories—U.S.—Direcs.
> Mineral Industries—Direcs.
> Museums—U.S.—Direcs.
> Regional Planners—U.S.—Direcs.
> Research—U.S.—Direcs.
> Sciences—U.S.—Information Services
> Universities and Colleges—U.S.—Direcs.

Use the *periodical indexes* to find current articles on employers' research interests or specialized directories, e.g.:

> Art Index
> Avery Architectural Index
> Engineering Index
> Public Affairs Information Service
> Science Citation Index

Following is a list of directories available in most career libraries.

GENERAL

American Council of Independent Laboratories, Directory, 15th Edition. Washington, D.C.: American Council of Independent Laboratories, 1978.

Subtitled "A guide to the leading independent, testing, research and inspection labs of America." A one-page description of each lab includes a history, specific services, and types of clientele.

Consultants and Consulting Organizations, ed. by Paul Wasserman, 3rd ed. Detroit, MI: Gale Research Co., 1982.

Facts about more than 5,000 firms and individuals that perform consulting work in a variety of fields.

Directory of Consultants, Spring 1978. Los Altos, CA: Professional and Technical Consultants Association, 1978.

Includes brief summary of each member's expertise and cross-index of members by consulting specialty.

Peterson's Annual Guide to Engineering, Science, and Computer Jobs. Princeton, NJ: Peterson's Guides, 1983.

Describes entry-level opportunities in all major segments of U.S. industry for technical bachelor's, master's and doctoral degree holders. Includes salary ranges, starting assignments, training, starting locations, international assignments, and summer programs.

Research Centers Directory, ed. by Archie M. Palmer. Detroit, MI: Gale Research Co., 1983.

CHEMISTRY AND PHYSICS

The Big 1000: The Major Employers of Chemical Technicians, Chemists, and Chemical Engineers. Chico, CA: The Employment Press, 1977.

This source is a listing of 1000 employers for people in the field of chemistry and chemical engineering. Section one is a listing of governmental contacts. Section two is comprised of manufacturers. Section three lists non-manufacturer employers.

Physical Sciences Jobs Handbook. Gaithersburg, MD: Prospect Press, 1981.

This guide was developed for specialists in earth and atmospheric sciences, chemistry, physics, computer science, mathematics, and statistics. Provides sources of job listings, job banks, and placement services. Provides lists of employers interested in science and math-related majors organized by employer type.

COMPUTER SCIENCE

Comp Job, 3rd ed. Chico, CA: Employment Information Services, 1979.

Lists the largest firms in the data processing industry as well as some selected medium and smaller-sized organizations. Includes a section on career guidance in the computer science field.

Peterson's Annual Guide to Engineering, Science, and Computer Jobs. Princeton, NJ: Peterson's Guides, 1983.

Describes entry-level opportunities in all major segments of U.S. industry for technical bachelor's, master's and doctoral degree holders. Includes salary ranges, starting assignments, training, starting locations, international assignments, and summer programs.

ENERGY AND ENVIRONMENTAL PROTECTION

California Environmental Directory: A Guide to Organizations and Resources, ed. by Thaddeus C. Tryzna. Claremont, CA: California Institute of Public Affairs, 1980.

Contains a "User's Guide" designed to assist readers in identifying organizations concerned with specific areas of interest. Contains alphabetically arranged sections on federal and California State agencies, other government units, citizens, professional, educational, and research organizations.

California Solar Business Directory, ed. by Jerry Yudelson and Margaret Kitchin. Sacramento, CA: Solar Business Office, 1980.

Includes information about California State programs and a listing of Solar Housing Developments in California. The directory lists California Solar Businesses alphabetically. Codes for each business indicate its particular specialty.

Center for Environmental Intern Programs 1982 Intern Directory. Boston, MA: Center for Environmental Intern Programs, 1982.

Provides names of interns who worked during the year of 1982 listed alphabetically. Contains index of internships by topic.

Conservation Directory. Washington, D.C.: National Wildlife Federation, 1982.

Lists organizations, agencies, and officials concerned with natural resources use management.

Energy Information Referral Directory. Washington, D.C.: U.S. Department of Energy, 1980.

Lists the office of primary interest for a particular activity in DOE or related agencies. The arrangement is topical (e.g., building and community systems, appropriate technology) and each subtopic is assigned an alphanumeric designation for use in accessing entries from the index.

Environmental Jobs Handbook. Mt. Airy, MD: Mikon Publishing Co., 1982.

Contains a discussion of environmental jobs in many fields and lists the various sources of these jobs. Includes federal opportunities, descriptions of private consultants, industrial firms, research centers, universities, and other employers. Also includes job search information.

Solar Energy and Research Directory. Ann Arbor, MI: Ann Arbor Science Publishers, Inc., 1977.

The entries of this directory are arranged according to major area of activity. The major classifications are as follows: Energy Conservation, manufacturers of solar components, manufacturers of solar total systems, distributors of solar products, design/construction of residences or buildings, solar research, solar energy—other related areas. Lists information about additional endeavors of each company as well as addresses, phone numbers, and names of possible contacts.

ENGINEERING

✓ *American Consulting Engineers Council (ACEC) 1983/84 Directory.* Washington, D.C.: American Consulting Engineers Council, August, 1983.

Lists ACEC member organizations with names and addresses of all officers and staff executives. Organized alphabetically by state.

1983 Directory & Membership Roster, Consulting Engineers Association of California. Burlingame, CA: Consulting Engineers Association of California, 1983.

Lists California Consulting Engineering firms alphabetically by firm name with number of employees and specialties. Includes roster of individual members and geographical distribution of member firms by discipline.

1984 U.S.A. Oil Industry Directory. Tulsa, OK: Penn Well Books, 1984.

Lists principal oil companies in the United States. Divided into sections as follows: integrated oil companies, large independent producers, drilling fund companies, pipeline transmission, marketing firms, associations, and government agencies.

LIFE SCIENCES

Life Sciences Jobs Handbook. Gaithersburg, MD: R.B. Uleck Associates, 1982.

Presents a variety of employer resources for life and other science majors. Includes a field identification and job search strategies for science majors.

Genetic Engineering News Guide to Biotechnology Companies. New York, NY: Mary Ann Liebert, Inc., 1983.

Biotechnology companies are listed alphabetically along with their addresses, phone numbers, company presidents, technologies and markets.

Worldwide Directory of National Earth-Science Agencies and Related International Organizations. Washington, D.C.: U.S. Department of the Interior, 1981.

Provides addresses of governmental earth-science agencies around the world that have functions similar to the U.S. Geological Survey. Also lists addresses of major international organizations that are concerned with some phase of the earth sciences. Arranged alphabetically by name of country.

INFORMATION OF SPECIAL INTEREST TO ETHNIC MINORITIES, WOMEN & THE PHYSICALLY DISABLED

Some *subject headings* to check to locate similar materials through a library's card catalog include:

Women's liberation movement

Minorities—Education—U.S.—Directories

Following is a list of directories in many career libraries:

The College Guide for Students with Disabilities. Cambridge, MA: Abt Books, 1976.

This guide, similar to general college guides, looks at all issues of interest to the disabled student thinking of going to college—the law, testing, financial aid, sources of learning aids and materials, publications, etc. There are detailed indices, and many charts showing if particular schools are physically accessible (classroom buildings and others). The charts do not discuss access for blind or deaf students; however, the descriptions will tell you what student services are available. Not all schools in the country are listed. Note that the guide is several years old and some information may be incorrect.

Directory of Career Resources for Minorities. Santa Monica, CA: Ready Reference Press, 1980.

Lists career resources and opportunities available to minorities. Includes private, non-profit minority organizations; social and community service agencies; college-affiliated resource centers, etc.

Directory of Career Resources for Women. Santa Monica, CA: Ready Reference Press, 1979.

Covers resources and opportunities for women offered by a wide variety of sources. Includes private, non-profit women's organizations; social and community service agencies; colleges' and universities' affiliated resource centers; independent consulting centers; YWCAs and others.

Directory of Special Programs for Minority Group Members, ed. by Willis Johnson. Garrett Park, MD: The Garrett Park Press, 1980.

Listings are sectioned by general employment and educational assistance programs: federally funded economic assistance job retraining, and student financial aid programs; college and university awards including special remedial, financial aid and other activities. Contains alphabetical and program type indexes.

Educators with Disabilities: A Resource Guide, by Joanne Gilmore, Diane Merchant, April Moore. Washington, D.C.: U.S. Government Printing Office, 1982.

A discussion of various disabilities with stories and anecdotes told by teachers and educators. Pictures illustrate how teachers are incorporated into classrooms of disabled and non-disabled students, how accommodations fit in. Section of recommendations and solutions of issues including career planning and certification. A 900-page directory follows, listing the resource educators, their degrees, specialties, and geographic locations.

Handicapped Funding Directory. Oceanside, NY: Research Grant Aides, 1982.

Information for planners and fund-seekers. Lists over 500 foundations, agencies, corporations, and associations which grant funds to institutions and agencies for programs and services for disabled people.

Handicapped Conditions and Services Directory. Detroit, MI: Gale Research Co., 1984.

Extensive listing, with descriptions of advocacy, consumer organizations, data banks, schools and a wide range of other organizations which dispense information about various disabilities, provide services to disabled people, technical assistance, etc. Useful index.

Internship Programs for Women, by Kathryn Mulligan. Washington, D.C.: Nat'l Society for Internships and Experiential Education, 1980.

Lists programs across the United States that provide internships for women. Includes each program's description and requirements.

Resource Directory of Handicapped Scientists. Washington, D.C.: American Association for the Advancement of Science, 1984.

Directory of people in the sciences nationwide. Lists name, address, phone number, scientific discipline, degree, most recent position, nature of disability, age when disabled, expertise, and interests for each scientist. Organized alphabetically by name. Includes geographic index.

Science for the Physically Handicapped in Higher Education: A Guide to Information. Springfield, VA: U.S. Dept. of Commerce, 1979.

Lists centers for information on careers in science and programs for disabled people. Includes where to write and what they do. Contains computerized data bases, associations, etc.

Index

About the Author

James I. Briggs has been Director of the Career Planning and Placement Center at the University of California-Berkeley since 1979. From 1973–1979, he was Director of the Center for Career Planning and Placement at Georgetown University. His experience in career development includes designing and teaching courses in career planning and job hunting for university students and career changers as well as conducting training programs for career counselors from high schools, colleges, and private and public sector organizations. He also teaches graduate students in the Career Development Program at John F. Kennedy University, Orinda, CA.

WHAT COLOR IS YOUR PARACHUTE?
by Richard N. Bolles

Based on the latest research this new completely revised and updated edition is designed to give the most practical step-by-step help imaginable to the career-changer or job-hunter whether he or she is sixteen or sixty-five. Questions dealt with are:

What methods of job-hunting and career-changing work best? What new methods have been developed by the best minds in the field? Is it possible to change jobs without going back for lengthy retraining?

6 × 9 inches, 400 pages, $8.95 paper, $14.95 cloth

THE THREE BOXES OF LIFE
by Richard N. Bolles

The three stages of our lives: education, then work, and then retirement, have tended to become three boxes for learning, achievement and leisure, argues Richard Bolles. Illustrating and giving substance to the instinctive feeling we all have about this, he proceeds to describe some very effective tools which everyone can use to blend learning, achieving, and playing during all the stages of our lives.

6 × 9 inches, 480 pages, $9.95 paper, $14.95 cloth

WHERE DO I GO FROM HERE WITH MY LIFE?
by John C. Crystal and Richard N. Bolles

New handy, smaller format/new cover for this perennial favorite—*the workbook* for the self-motivated individual student or professional who has an interest in a systematic approach to career planning bringing together two of the leaders in the field.

7 × 9 inches, 272 pages, $9.95 paper

DON'T USE A RESUME
by Richard Lathrop

This brief book is based on the methods and the section in *Who's Hiring Who* dealing with an alternative to the resume, *The Qualifications Brief*.

6 × 9 inches, 64 pages, $1.95 paper

You will find them in your bookstore or library, or you can order directly from us. Please include $1.00 additional for each book's shipping and handling.

TEN SPEED PRESS
P.O. Box 7123
Berkeley, California 94707